WILLIAMS-SONOMA

Small Plates

GENERAL EDITOR

Chuck Williams

RECIPES

Joanne Weir

PHOTOGRAPHY

Joyce Oudkerk Pool

TIME-LIFE BOOKS

Time-Life Books is a division of Time Life Inc.
Time-Life is a trademark of Time Warner Inc. U.S.A.

TIME-LIFE CUSTOM PUBLISHING
Vice President and Publisher: Terry Newell
Vice President of Sales and Marketing: Neil Levin
Director of Financial Operations: J. Brian Birky
Director of Acquisitions: Jennifer L. Pearce

WILLIAMS-SONOMA
Founder and Vice-Chairman: Chuck Williams
Associate Book Buyer: Cecilia Michaelis

WELDON OWEN INC.
President: John Owen
Vice President and Publisher: Wendely Harvey
Chief Operating Officer: Larry Partington
Vice President International Sales: Stuart Laurence
Series Editor: Val Cipollone
Managing Editor: Jan Newberry
Consulting Editor: Norman Kolpas
Copy Editor: Sharon Silva
Series Design: Kari Perin, Perin+Perin
Book Design: Diane Dempsey
Production Director: Stephanie Sherman
Production Manager: Christine DePedro
Production Editor: Sarah Lemas
Food Stylist: Andrea Lucich
Prop Stylist: Rebecca Stephany
Studio Assistant: Arjen Kammeraad
Food Styling Assistant: Elisabet der Nederlanden
Glossary Illustrations: Alice Harth

A NOTE ON WEIGHTS AND MEASURES

All recipes include customary U.S. and metric measurements. Metric conversions are based on a standard developed for these books and have been rounded off. Actual weights may vary.

The Williams-Sonoma Lifestyles Series
conceived and produced by Weldon Owen Inc.
814 Montgomery Street, San Francisco, CA 94133

In collaboration with Williams-Sonoma
3250 Van Ness Avenue, San Francisco, CA 94109

Separations by Colourscan Overseas Co. Pte. Ltd.
Printed in Singapore by Tien Wah Press (Pte.) Ltd.

A WELDON OWEN PRODUCTION

First printed in 1999
10 9 8 7 6 5 4 3 2 1

Library of Congress
Cataloging-in-Publication Data

Weir, Joanne.
Small plates / general editor, Chuck Williams;
recipes by Joanne Weir; photography by
Joyce Oudkerk Pool.
p. cm. — (Williams-Sonoma lifestyles)
Includes index.
ISBN 0-7370-2026-1
1. Cookery, International. I. Williams, Chuck.
II. Title. III. Series.
TX725.A1W375 1999
641.59— dc21 99-10021
CIP

A NOTE ON NUTRITIONAL ANALYSIS

Each recipe is analyzed for significant nutrients per serving. Not included in the analysis are ingredients that are optional or added to taste, or are suggested as an alternative or substitution either in the recipe or in the recipe introduction or accompanying tip. In recipes that yield a range of servings, the analysis is for the middle of that range.

Contents

Welcome

On my many trips to Europe over the years I've always enjoyed dining casually in the Mediterranean countries. Whether in a Spanish tapas bar, an Italian trattoria, or a Greek taverna, these informal meals always begin, and often center on, small plates of different foods that offer a wide variety of exciting tastes. That variety, together with the local drinks, never fails to spark lively conversation and a good time for all.

Meals composed of these small plates, whether called tapas, antipasti, or mezes, have become a popular way to entertain. With that in mind, I asked Mediterranean cooking expert Joanne Weir to develop the 47 recipes in this book. Arranged in chapters by country or region of origin, they provide a varied assortment of easy-to-make dishes from which to compose a buffet, a sit-down dinner party, or even a quick family meal. On the introductory pages, you'll find guidelines for preparing and serving small plates and the beverages that go with them. An illustrated glossary explains special ingredients and equipment.

All these features share one goal: to help you enjoy, and share with family and friends, these classic tastes from the Mediterranean.

Enjoying Small Plates at Home

Meals composed of small plates naturally call for a casual style of service, often in the form of a buffet. Match your utensils (above) to the particular recipes you have chosen, and use an equally appropriate array of large platters and bowls (right), as well as individual plates for your guests.

A Mediterranean Tradition

Throughout the countries that border the Mediterranean Sea, casual restaurants take pride in offering many small plates of different foods along with drinks, serving them either to start a meal or to be enjoyed as a meal in their own right. Spanish *tabernas, tascas,* or tapas bars might feature garlic-and-saffron-scented mussels, turnovers stuffed with sausage and olives, or thick wedges of onion-and-egg omelet. In Italy, an antipasto table at a trattoria could include anything from simple slices of grilled bread topped with fresh tomatoes to salads of fava (broad) beans and cheese to deep-fried fingers of polenta. A Turkish *lokanta* or Greek taverna might present such selections as skewers of grilled poultry or meat, tahini-enriched dips of puréed chickpeas (garbanzo beans), or rice-stuffed grape leaves.

As varied as these dishes may be, they all share a reliance on the finest seasonal ingredients, lively seasonings intended to sharpen the appetite, simple preparation techniques, and an unpretentious style of service. Such characteristics make it easy for home cooks to prepare these small plates in their own kitchens.

All of the recipes in this book, while true to the restaurant traditions of their origins, have been expressly developed to work in home kitchens. In some cases, you may find that they call for special ingredients or equipment (see Glossary, page 108), but these can be readily found in well-stocked food stores, ethnic markets, or kitchenware shops.

Serving Small Plates

A meal of small plates is ideal for a variety of occasions, from a hurried weeknight family supper to a special Saturday dinner party to a casual holiday buffet. You can limit your menu to dishes from one particular region, a Spanish tapas party, for example, or a simple spread of Italian antipasti. But there's no reason not to combine plates from different cuisines. Warm Shrimp Salad with Salsa Verde (page 46) from Italy served alongside Artichokes Stewed with Lemon and Garlic (page 88) from Greece and Spicy Pork Kabobs with Moorish Flavors (page 27) from Spain would make a fine crosscultural feast.

Pay close attention to the temperature at which various dishes are to be served. Some you might think would be set out hot are, in fact, traditionally offered at room temperature, such as Mushrooms Cooked with Garlic and Saffron (page 20). Many deep-fried dishes like Mozzarella in Carrozza (page 49) are best appreciated piping hot, but others, including Albóndigas (page 31) and Fennel Frittata (page 59), may be eaten hot, warm, or at room temperature.

Whether serving a family supper, a festive buffet, or a dinner party for friends, round out your menu of small plates with a selection of traditional beverages (see pages 14–15) and a typical dessert. For the latter, consider such simple preparations as a silky flan with Spanish tapas, gelato or granita and biscotti with Italian antipasti, or bakery-bought baklava with Greek or Middle Eastern mezes. Or set out an array of seasonal fresh fruits for an utterly easy—and satisfying—finish.

Planning for Spontaneity

A well-stocked pantry (above) is the key to successful entertaining. Look to ethnic markets and quality food stores for a wide variety of authentic ingredients to keep on hand. Many of these items can be served as small plates in their own right, including crisp bread sticks, sliced bread, cheeses, olives, and cured meats (above, right).

Stocking the Pantry

One of the reasons Mediterranean-style small plates are so appealing is their spontaneous character—the impression that they are prepared at the spur of the moment, using ingredients that are on hand. As any good cook knows, however, the ability to cook spontaneously depends in large part on having a pantry stocked with staples. (You'll find many pantry items explained in detail in the glossary entries on pages 108–111.)

Well-stocked food stores today carry most if not all of the ingredients you'll need to compose a menu of small plates. You might also look for them in ethnic markets or specialty-food shops.

Three key ingredients are sometimes referred to as the holy trinity of Mediterranean kitchens: olive oil, garlic, and tomatoes. Pure olive oil is used as a cooking fat, while extra-virgin olive oil is often called for as an essential flavoring element, conveying the rich, sweet taste of the fruit from which it is pressed. Garlic is prized for the pungent bite it adds to many savory dishes. And tomatoes, fresh in summertime and canned year-round, contribute their full, sweet taste, bright red color, and substantial body to salads, sauces, and toppings alike.

A good selection of herbs and spices also expands the repertoire of the small-plates cook. All of those called for in this book are readily available dried in the seasonings sections of food stores or, in the case of fresh herbs, in produce sections and at farmers' markets.

Beyond these staples, always shop with seasonality in mind. Seek out the freshest, finest produce, meats, poultry, and seafood, letting their availability and quality dictate the menus you plan.

Ready-to-Serve Items

When shopping, keep an eye out for the kind of ready-to-serve foods that are also frequently offered on their own throughout the Mediterranean. These are excellent complements to any small-plates menu. Olives, whether green or black, cured with brine or salt, marinated in vinegar or oil, and seasoned in various ways, may be served in small bowls or plates. Be sure to set out little saucers in which guests can discard the olive pits.

Fried or roasted and seasoned nuts are another popular inclusion, particularly almonds, walnuts, and in Greece and the Middle East, pistachio nuts.

Cheeses, an ingredient in many dishes and an important part of the small-plates pantry, are also good choices for serving on their own. Try cubes of Greek or Turkish feta, Italian Parmesan, and Spanish manchego.

Good bread is a vital part of any menu that features small plates. Choose rustic Italian loaves, crusty baguettes, crunchy bread sticks, or crackers to serve with the recipes in this book. If your menu includes Middle Eastern dishes, put some warmed pita bread on the table, or try making a batch of the Crisp Pita Chips at right.

CRISP PITA CHIPS

2 pita bread rounds, each 8 inches (20 cm) in diameter
3 tablespoons extra-virgin olive oil
salt to taste

❋ Preheat an oven to 375°F (190°C).

❋ Split each pita bread into 2 rounds by carefully separating it along the outside seam. Cut each round into 6–8 wedges. Spread the wedges on a baking sheet. Drizzle with the olive oil, sprinkle with salt, and toss to coat evenly. Spread out the wedges in a single layer.

❋ Bake, turning the wedges occasionally, until crisp, 10–12 minutes. Remove from the oven and let cool completely on the baking sheet before storing.

MAKES 24–32 CHIPS; SERVES 6

Traditional Techniques

Frying, grilling, and working with yeast doughs and filo sheets are some of the cooking techniques you'll encounter in this book. The following tips will help to ensure success with your small plates.

DEEP-FRYING RICE CROQUETTES (RECIPE ON PAGE 60)

1. For successful deep-frying use a thermometer to be sure your oil is heated to the correct temperature. If the oil is too cool, your croquettes will be greasy; if too hot, they may burn.

2. Fry just a few croquettes at a time. Crowding the pan will reduce the temperature of the oil. Drain them on a cooling rack set over a paper towel–lined tray, to help keep them crisp.

BAKING PIZZA AND FOCACCIA (RECIPES ON PAGES 54 AND 71)

1. To test whether your dough is fully risen, poke it gently with your finger. If an indentation remains, it's ready to be punched down and shaped into rounds.

2. A baker's peel makes it easy to transfer the dough to and from the hot oven. Baking on a pizza stone helps ensure that the bread will be crisp and evenly browned.

GRILLING KABOBS (RECIPES ON PAGES 27, 83, AND 90)

1. If using wooden skewers, be sure to soak them in water to cover for at least 20 minutes before using to keep them from burning. Thread the ingredients onto the skewers just before you're ready to grill.

2. Wait until your coals are covered with white ash, a sign that they are sufficiently hot, before you begin grilling. Cook the kabobs just until they are well browned on the surface, but still juicy inside, 10–15 minutes.

WORKING WITH FILO DOUGH (RECIPE ON PAGE 72)

1. For easy handling, let filo dough stand at room temperature for 2 hours before unfolding. Cover the sheets with a lightly dampened towel to prevent them from drying out. Brushing each layer of dough with butter ensures it will be crisp when baked.

2. Filo dough is wrapped around filling to produce pastry packages of many different shapes. To make the turnovers known as tiropites, fold the filled strips over diagonally to form a triangle, then continue folding in a triangle until you reach the end.

Beverages

Sparkling and full-bodied red wines (top) pair well with many small plates. For something a bit more unusual, try the beverages each Mediterranean country serves with their small plates. In Italy, for example, a refreshingly bitter mix of Campari and soda sometimes starts a meal, while Greek tavernas customarily pour anise-flavored ouzo diluted with water (above). Spanish tapas, it is said, evolved as accompaniments to dry sherry (near right), although in summer they are sometimes paired with a glass of sangria (far right).

Making Traditional Choices

In their countries of origin, small plates and refreshing beverages are inseparable. When you plan to serve such dishes, bear in mind the drinks with which they are customarily served. At the same time, you can mix and match drinks and dishes from different regions.

SPAIN. Spanish tapas came about as complements to sherry, and good-quality examples of that fortified wine remain the classic accompaniments. Chilled dry and medium-dry sherries go well with many savory dishes. If you prefer regular wine, seek out one of the many excellent lighter Spanish varieties such as sparkling Cava or a white such as Albariño. One of the most refreshing drinks to serve with small plates is the popular red-wine punch known as sangria (recipe, opposite).

ITALY. In Italy, small plates are sometimes served with a bitter *aperitivo* such as Campari, mixed with a splash of soda or with sweet vermouth and gin to make

a Negroni. More often, a dry sparkling wine such as Asti Spumante Brut or Prosecco might be poured, perhaps flavored with a purée of white peaches to make a Bellini. Also popular are light white wines typified by Orvieto, Pinot Grigio, Pinot Bianco, and Tokai.

GREECE AND THE MIDDLE EAST. Further east, small plates are traditionally washed down with the anise-flavored spirit known in Greece as ouzo and in Turkey as raki, served diluted with cold water in a tall glass. Well-chilled local beers or lighter white versions of the resinated Greek wine known as retsina may also be poured.

Offering Other Options

Feel free to pour any other favorite alcoholic beverages that suit the small plates you serve. Many nonalcoholic beverages are also traditionally offered with small plates, from sparkling waters and fruit juices to both regional and internationally known soft drinks. Be sure to provide some of these as an option for your guests.

SANGRIA

Make this classic Spanish punch at least 4 hours in advance to allow time for the flavors to blend.

2 bottles (24 fl oz/750 ml each) full-bodied red wine
½ cup (4 fl oz/125 ml) orange juice
2 tablespoons orange liqueur such as Gran Torres or Grand Marnier (optional)
1½ tablespoons sugar
2 small oranges, halved lengthwise and cut crosswise into slices ½ inch (12 mm) thick
1 lemon, cut crosswise into slices ½ inch (12 mm) thick
12 red or green seedless grapes, halved lengthwise
2 small peaches, pitted and cut into wedges ½ inch (12 mm) thick
9 strawberries, stems removed and halved lengthwise
2 cups (16 fl oz/500 ml) sparkling water, chilled
ice cubes

❀ In a large glass pitcher, combine the wine, orange juice, orange liqueur (if using), and sugar. Stir well to dissolve the sugar. Stir in the orange and lemon slices and the grapes. Cover and refrigerate for at least 4 hours or up to overnight.

❀ Just before serving, add the peach wedges, strawberries, sparkling water, and ice cubes to the pitcher. Stir well, then pour into balloon wineglasses to serve.

SERVES 6–8

Planning Menus

The recipes in this book can be combined in a wide variety of ways to make interesting small-plates menus. The 10 suggestions that appear here represent only a handful of the possible combinations. When planning your menu, take advantage of what produce is at its peak in the market. Consider whether the recipes can be made ahead, as well as the temperature at which they should be served. Keep in mind the need for diversity of ingredients, creating menus in which the foods and flavors complement one another. Finally, see pages 14 and 15 for tips on beverages to serve alongside your tapas, antipasti, and mezes.

Winter Menu

Caramelized Onion Tortilla
PAGE 24

Chickpeas Stewed with Chorizo
PAGE 35

Empanaditas
PAGE 39

Rioja

Simple Fare

Chilled Mussels with Tomatoes and Sherry Vinegar
PAGE 40

Coarse Country Bread

Sherry

Hearty Middle Eastern

Grilled Lamb Kabobs with Mint-Yogurt Sauce
PAGE 90

Green Beans Stewed with Tomatoes and Garlic
PAGE 99

Crisp Pita Chips
PAGE 11

The Best of Italy

Caponata
PAGE 56

Crostini with Sweet-and-Sour Chicken Livers
PAGE 62

White Bean Salad with Red, Green, and Yellow Peppers
PAGE 69

Greek Sampler

Spinach Tiropites
PAGE 72

Grape Leaves Stuffed with Rice and Currants
PAGE 76

Chicken Souvlaki
PAGE 83

Ouzo

Springtime Antipasti

Fava Beans with Pecorino, Olive Oil, and Lemon
PAGE 45

Warm Shrimp Salad with Salsa Verde
PAGE 46

Campari and Soda

Vegetarian Mezes

Yogurt Dip with Garlic, Mint, and Dill
PAGE 85

Saganaki
PAGE 86

Artichokes Stewed with Lemon and Garlic
PAGE 88

Tapas Grill

Grilled Bread with Ripe Tomatoes and Olive Oil
PAGE 19

Spicy Pork Kabobs with Moorish Flavors
PAGE 27

Catalan Mixed Grilled Vegetables
PAGE 36

International Feast

Albóndigas
PAGE 31

Bite-Sized Rice Croquettes
PAGE 60

Turkish Tomato and Chile Relish
PAGE 96

Dips and Salads

Hummus
PAGE 93

Tabbouleh
PAGE 94

Baba Ghanoush
PAGE 100

Pita Bread

Grilled Bread with Ripe Tomatoes and Olive Oil

PREP TIME: 15 MINUTES

COOKING TIME: 5 MINUTES, PLUS PREPARING FIRE

INGREDIENTS

2 cloves garlic

coarse salt

¼ cup (2 fl oz/60 ml) extra-virgin olive oil

12 slices coarse country bread, each about ¾ inch (2 cm) thick

3 very ripe tomatoes, halved crosswise

ground pepper to taste

FOR THE OPTIONAL GARNISHES

½ cup (2½ oz/75 g) green or black brine-cured olives, pitted and slivered

6 paper-thin slices serrano ham *(see note)*

12 paper-thin slices manchego cheese

SERVING TIP: Served the grilled bread immediately, before it absorbs the olive oil and becomes soggy.

During tomato season, Spanish cooks prepare this simple dish of juicy ripe tomatoes, fragrant oil, and country bread. If possible, seek out Spain's famed air-cured serrano ham for the most traditional flavor, although Italian prosciutto or French Bayonne ham can be substituted. Prepare this dish when you're grilling other foods. You can toast the bread under a broiler, but grilling gives it the best flavor.

SERVES 6

❃ Prepare a medium-hot fire in a charcoal grill.

❃ In a mortar, combine the garlic and salt to taste. Mash together with a pestle to form a paste. Mix in the olive oil.

❃ Place the bread slices on the grill rack 4–5 inches (10–13 cm) from the fire and grill, turning once, until golden brown, 30–60 seconds on each side. Transfer the bread slices to a platter. Cupping a tomato half in your palm, rub it over the top sides of 2 pieces of toast, squeezing slightly to leave a smear of pulp, seeds, and juice on the surface. Repeat with the remaining tomato halves and bread. Drizzle the olive oil–garlic mixture evenly over the bread slices and sprinkle with pepper. Serve immediately with the optional garnishes arranged on top, if desired.

NUTRITIONAL ANALYSIS PER SERVING: Calories 257 (Kilojoules 1,079); Protein 6 g; Carbohydrates 33 g; Total Fat 12 g; Saturated Fat 2 g; Cholesterol 0 mg; Sodium 356 mg; Dietary Fiber 3 g

Mushrooms Cooked with Garlic and Saffron

PREP TIME: 20 MINUTES

COOKING TIME: 45 MINUTES, PLUS MARINATING OVERNIGHT

INGREDIENTS

1 cup (8 fl oz/250 ml) dry white wine

1 cup (8 fl oz/250 ml) white wine vinegar

¼ cup (2 fl oz/60 ml) extra-virgin olive oil

12 cloves garlic, thinly sliced

4 bay leaves

¼ teaspoon red pepper flakes

large pinch of saffron threads

2 teaspoons salt

1 teaspoon ground black pepper

2½ lb (1.25 kg) fresh small button mushrooms, brushed clean

1 tablespoon chopped fresh flat-leaf (Italian) parsley

PREP TIP: To clean mushrooms, lightly brush them with a soft kitchen towel or a mushroom brush. Do not rinse them with water, as they will absorb too much moisture and be less flavorful.

In the fall and again in the spring, Spain's markets are flooded with wild mushrooms, which are commonly simmered with garlic and other seasonings. Here, small button mushrooms are substituted with excellent results.

SERVES 6

❁ In a saucepan, combine the wine, vinegar, olive oil, garlic, bay leaves, red pepper flakes, saffron, salt, and black pepper. Place over high heat and bring to a boil. Reduce the heat to medium-low, cover, and simmer until the liquid thickens slightly and forms a flavorful stock, about 30 minutes. Remove from the heat and pour through a fine-mesh sieve placed over a bowl, pressing against the contents of the sieve with the back of a wooden spoon to extract as much liquid as possible. Return the liquid to the saucepan. Discard the solids.

❁ Add the mushrooms to the liquid in the saucepan along with enough water almost to cover them. Bring to a boil over high heat, reduce the heat to medium-low, and simmer uncovered, stirring occasionally, until the mushrooms are tender, about 3 minutes. Using a slotted spoon, transfer the mushrooms to a bowl. Place the cooking liquid over high heat and boil, uncovered, until reduced to ½ cup (4 fl oz/125 ml), 5–10 minutes. Pour the hot liquid over the mushrooms, mix well, and let cool completely. Cover and refrigerate overnight.

❁ About 30 minutes before serving, remove the mushrooms from the refrigerator and bring to room temperature. Garnish with the parsley and serve.

NUTRITIONAL ANALYSIS PER SERVING: Calories 146 (Kilojoules 613); Protein 4 g; Carbohydrates 13 g; Total Fat 10 g; Saturated Fat 1 g; Cholesterol 0 mg; Sodium 788 mg; Dietary Fiber 3 g

Green Olive and Manchego Puffs

PREP TIME: 35 MINUTES, PLUS 1 HOUR FOR RESTING

COOKING TIME: 15 MINUTES

INGREDIENTS

1 cup (5 oz/155 g) all-purpose (plain) flour

¼ teaspoon red pepper flakes

3 eggs

¾ cup (6 fl oz/180 ml) beer, at room temperature

2 tablespoons olive oil

½ teaspoon salt

pinch of ground black pepper

peanut or corn oil for deep-frying

10 oz (315 g) chorizo sausages, casings removed

½ cup (2 oz/60 g) grated manchego or Parmesan cheese

⅓ cup (2 oz/60 g) Spanish brine-cured green olives, pitted and chopped

3 tablespoons chopped fresh flat-leaf (Italian) parsley

MAKE-AHEAD TIP: The batter can be prepared 1 day in advance, but do not add the egg whites. Cover and store in the refrigerator. Thirty minutes before serving, bring the batter to room temperature, whip the egg whites, and proceed with the recipe.

Spaniards have an affinity for sausages, and they make many different kinds. But the most popular type is undoubtedly chorizo, made from pork and heavily spiced with cumin, garlic, and paprika. The last is what gives the sausage its deep red color. In this recipe, chorizo is combined with green olives in crisp deep-fried fritters. Manchego cheese, a hard, ivory to pale gold sheep's milk cheese from La Mancha, is available at most fine cheese shops.

MAKES ABOUT 30 PUFFS; SERVES 6

❋ Sift the flour into a bowl. Add the red pepper flakes and stir to mix well. Make a well in the center.. Separate the eggs, placing the yolks in a small bowl and the whites in a medium bowl. Beat the yolks with a fork just until blended and pour into the well in the flour. Add the beer, olive oil, salt, and black pepper. Using a spoon, mix well, but do not overmix or the batter will get stringy. Cover and let stand at room temperature for 1 hour.

❋ In a deep, heavy saucepan, pour in oil to a depth of 2 inches (5 cm) and heat to 375°F (190°C) on a deep-frying thermometer.

❋ While the oil is heating, place the chorizo in a frying pan over medium heat and break it up with a wooden spoon. Cook, stirring occasionally, until heated through, 3–4 minutes. At the same time, using an electric mixer, beat the egg whites until stiff peaks form.

❋ Fold the egg whites, chorizo, cheese, olives, and chopped parsley into the batter. Working in batches, drop the batter by heaping tablespoonfuls into the hot oil; do not crowd the pan. Fry, turning occasionally, until golden, 2–3 minutes. Using a slotted spoon, transfer to paper towels to drain. Keep warm.

❋ Arrange the puffs on a warmed platter and serve immediately.

NUTRITIONAL ANALYSIS PER SERVING: Calories 498 (Kilojoules 2,092); Protein 20 g; Carbohydrates 21 g; Total Fat 36 g; Saturated Fat 11 g; Cholesterol 156 mg; Sodium 1,098 mg; Dietary Fiber 1 g

Caramelized Onion Tortilla

PREP TIME: 20 MINUTES

COOKING TIME: 1¾ HOURS

INGREDIENTS

4 tablespoons (2 fl oz/60 ml) olive oil

3 lb (1.5 kg) yellow onions, finely chopped

6 eggs

salt and ground pepper to taste

fresh sage leaves (optional)

This Spanish tortilla is a cousin to the Italian frittata. In Spain, it is called a *tortilla de cebolla,* as opposed to the more common *tortilla española* made with potatoes. Like all tortillas, however, it is cut into wedges for serving. This recipe calls for a generous amount of onions, which become sweeter during long cooking.

SERVES 6

❁ In a frying pan over medium heat, warm 2 tablespoons of the olive oil. Add the onions and stir to combine. Cover and cook until softened, about 15 minutes, stirring once halfway through. Uncover, stir, and reduce the heat to low. Re-cover and continue to cook, stirring occasionally, until very soft and golden, about 1 hour. Remove from the heat and let cool for 10 minutes.

❁ In a bowl, whisk together the eggs, salt, and pepper until blended. Stir in the onions.

❁ In a 10-inch (25-cm) nonstick frying pan over medium heat, warm the remaining 2 tablespoons oil just until it begins to smoke. Pour the egg-onion mixture into the pan and cook, occasionally loosening the edges with a spatula to allow the uncooked portion to run underneath and to form a high, rounded edge. When the eggs are almost set, after 10–12 minutes, invert a plate over the top of the frying pan. Holding them together firmly, flip the plate and pan so the tortilla falls onto the plate. Slide the tortilla back into the frying pan, browned side up. Cook until browned on the bottom, 4–5 minutes. It should be slightly soft in the center.

❁ Slide the tortilla out onto a serving plate. Let stand for 10 minutes, then cut into wedges. Serve hot, warm, or at room temperature. Garnish with sage leaves, if you like.

NUTRITIONAL ANALYSIS PER SERVING: Calories 240 (Kilojoules 1,008); Protein 9 g; Carbohydrates 20 g; Total Fat 14 g; Saturated Fat 3 g; Cholesterol 213 mg; Sodium 70 mg; Dietary Fiber 4 g

Spicy Pork Kabobs with Moorish Flavors

PREP TIME: 35 MINUTES, PLUS 2 HOURS FOR MARINATING

COOKING TIME: 15 MINUTES, PLUS PREPARING FIRE

INGREDIENTS

2 cloves garlic, thinly sliced

1 teaspoon salt

1 teaspoon coriander seeds

1 teaspoon paprika

¾ teaspoon cumin seeds

½ teaspoon dried thyme

¼ teaspoon red pepper flakes

ground black pepper to taste

3 tablespoons olive oil

1 tablespoon lemon juice

1 tablespoon chopped fresh flat-leaf (Italian) parsley

1 lb (500 g) lean pork, cut into ¾–1-inch (2–2.5-cm) cubes

lemon wedges

SERVING TIP: You can serve this tapa as a light main course. Accompany with grilled vegetables and saffron-seasoned rice.

The Moors invaded Spain in the eighth century and remained for 500 years. Of Berber and Arab descent, they left their influence on every aspect of Spanish life, including the kitchen. This recipe shows their legacy in its heavy use of spices. Lamb can be substituted for the pork.

SERVES 6

❂ In a mortar, combine the garlic with ¼ teaspoon of the salt. Mash together with a pestle to form a paste. In a dry frying pan over high heat, combine the coriander seeds, paprika, cumin seeds, thyme, and red pepper flakes. Heat, shaking the pan occasionally, until hot and fragrant, about 30 seconds. Transfer the mixture to a spice grinder and grind to a fine powder.

❂ In a bowl, stir together the garlic paste, ground spices, the remaining ¾ teaspoon salt, the black pepper, olive oil, lemon juice, and parsley. Add the pork cubes and turn to coat well. Cover and let stand at cool room temperature for 2 hours, stirring occasionally.

❂ Prepare a medium-hot fire in a charcoal grill. At the same time, put 12 bamboo skewers in water to cover.

❂ Remove the pork cubes from the marinade, reserving the marinade, and drain the skewers. Thread the pork cubes onto the skewers, dividing the cubes evenly among them. In a small pan, bring the reserved marinade to a boil over high heat and boil for about 3 minutes. Remove from the heat. Place the kabobs on the grill rack 4–5 inches (10–13 cm) from the fire and grill, basting occasionally with the reserved marinade and turning every 2–3 minutes, until browned but still juicy, 10–15 minutes.

❂ Transfer to a warmed platter and garnish with lemon wedges. Serve immediately.

NUTRITIONAL ANALYSIS PER SERVING: Calories 262 (Kilojoules 1,100); Protein 14 g; Carbohydrates 1 g; Total Fat 22 g; Saturated Fat 6 g; Cholesterol 53 mg; Sodium 427 mg; Dietary Fiber 0 g

Crisp Potatoes with Allioli

PREP TIME: 20 MINUTES

COOKING TIME: 55 MINUTES

INGREDIENTS

3 lb (1.5 kg) small red potatoes, unpeeled

1 tablespoon olive oil

salt and ground pepper to taste

FOR THE ALLIOLI

½ cup (4 fl oz/125 ml) olive oil

½ cup (4 fl oz/125 ml) vegetable, safflower, or corn oil

1 egg yolk

4 cloves garlic, minced

2 tablespoons white wine vinegar

coarse salt and ground pepper to taste

1–2 tablespoons warm water

SERVING TIP: The allioli is also delicious stirred into a puréed soup or served with grilled fish.

Catalan allioli is the Iberian equivalent of Provençal aioli, or garlic mayonnaise. Drizzled over hot, crisp potatoes, it melts into them, creating a rich, creamy sauce. Sometimes a spicy-hot tomato sauce is used to dress potatoes, in which case they are called *patatas bravas,* or "brave potatoes."

SERVES 6

❁ Position a rack in the upper third of an oven and preheat to 375°F (190°C).

❁ Halve the potatoes crosswise and place in a baking dish large enough to hold them in a single layer. Drizzle with the olive oil and sprinkle with salt and pepper. Toss to coat evenly, then arrange in a single layer. Bake until golden, tender, and crispy, 45–55 minutes.

❁ Meanwhile, make the allioli: In a small bowl, combine the two oils. In another bowl, whisk together the egg yolk and 1 tablespoon of the combined oils until an emulsion forms. Drop by drop, add the remaining oil mixture to the egg emulsion, always whisking constantly. Do not add the oil too quickly, and be sure that the emulsion is set before adding more oil. Season with the garlic, vinegar, coarse salt, and pepper. Whisking constantly, add as much of the warm water as needed to create a smooth, thick consistency.

❁ To serve, place the potatoes on a serving platter and pour half of the allioli over the top. (Cover and refrigerate the remaining allioli and reserve for another use.) Serve immediately.

NUTRITIONAL ANALYSIS PER SERVING: Calories 537 (Kilojoules 2,255); Protein 5 g; Carbohydrates 42 g; Total Fat 40 g; Saturated Fat 5 g; Cholesterol 35 mg; Sodium 19 mg; Dietary Fiber 4 g

Albóndigas

PREP TIME: 45 MINUTES

COOKING TIME: 35 MINUTES

INGREDIENTS

FOR THE MEATBALLS

¾ lb (375 g) ground (minced) pork

¾ lb (375 g) ground (minced) veal

1 cup (4 oz/125 g) fine dried bread crumbs

4 cloves garlic, minced

2 tablespoons chopped fresh flat-leaf (Italian) parsley

1½ teaspoons ground coriander

¾ teaspoon salt

½ teaspoon ground black pepper

½ teaspoon ground cumin

pinch of cayenne pepper

FOR THE SAUCE

3 tablespoons olive oil

1 yellow onion, minced

2 cloves garlic, minced

3 cups (18 oz/560 g) peeled, seeded, and chopped tomatoes (fresh or canned)

1 cup (8 fl oz/250 ml) dry white wine

½ teaspoon salt

½ teaspoon ground black pepper

COOKING TIP: The albóndigas can also be made with ground beef or lamb in place of pork and veal.

Albóndigas, small meatballs made all over Spain, are among the most common tapas served both at bars and in homes. When made very small, they are added to soups, and when formed into larger balls, they are substantial enough to serve as a main course.

SERVES 6

❋ Preheat an oven to 350°F (180°C).

❋ To make the meatballs, in a bowl, combine the pork, veal, bread crumbs, garlic, parsley, coriander, salt, black pepper, cumin, and cayenne. Mix well. Form the mixture into about 30 balls, each about 1 inch (2.5 cm) in diameter. As the balls are formed, place on an ungreased baking sheet.

❋ Bake until almost firm to the touch, 10–12 minutes. Remove from the oven and set aside.

❋ Meanwhile, make the sauce: In a frying pan over medium heat, warm the olive oil. Add the onion and garlic and cook, stirring occasionally, until soft, about 7 minutes. Add the tomatoes and wine and simmer slowly, until thickened, about 15 minutes.

❋ Add the meatballs, salt, and pepper and continue to simmer slowly until the sauce thickens and the meatballs are cooked through, about 10 minutes.

❋ Transfer to a bowl and serve hot, warm, or at room temperature.

NUTRITIONAL ANALYSIS PER SERVING: Calories 403 (Kilojoules 1,693); Protein 24 g; Carbohydrates 22 g; Total Fat 24 g; Saturated Fat 7 g; Cholesterol 87 mg; Sodium 737 mg; Dietary Fiber 3 g

Sizzling Garlic Shrimp with Sherry

PREP TIME: 20 MINUTES

COOKING TIME: 5 MINUTES

INGREDIENTS

3 tablespoons extra-virgin olive oil

6 cloves garlic, thinly sliced

pinch of red pepper flakes

1¼ lb (625 g) shrimp (prawns), peeled and deveined

½ teaspoon pimentón (optional)

⅓ cup (3 fl oz/80 ml) dry sherry

salt and ground black pepper to taste

1½ teaspoons chopped fresh flat-leaf (Italian) parsley

SERVING TIP: This dish is also delicious served with Albariño, a fruity wine from northwestern Spain.

Serve these succulent shrimp piping hot in a *cazuela,* a traditional terra-cotta baking dish, with lots of crusty bread for sopping up the delicious juices. Pimentón, smoked, dried, and ground pimiento pepper, is available at Spanish markets and specialty-food stores. Choose a good-quality amontillado, dry oloroso, or fino sherry for cooking and sipping.

SERVES 6

❁ In a large frying pan over medium-high heat, warm the olive oil. Add the garlic and red pepper flakes and cook, stirring, for 15 seconds. Add the shrimp and the pimentón, if using, and cook, stirring, until the shrimp curl and turn pink, about 3 minutes. Add the sherry and continue to cook until the sherry is reduced by half, about 1 minute. Season with salt and black pepper.

❁ Transfer to a serving dish and garnish with the parsley. Serve immediately.

NUTRITIONAL ANALYSIS PER SERVING: Calories 162 (Kilojoules 680); Protein 16 g; Carbohydrates 2 g; Total Fat 8 g; Saturated Fat 1 g; Cholesterol 116 mg; Sodium 115 mg; Dietary Fiber 0 g

Chickpeas Stewed with Chorizo

PREP TIME: 30 MINUTES, PLUS 4 HOURS FOR SOAKING

COOKING TIME: 1¾ HOURS

INGREDIENTS

2 cups (14 oz/440 g) dried chickpeas (garbanzo beans)

¼ teaspoon ground cloves

¼ teaspoon ground cinnamon

1 bay leaf

large pinch of dried thyme

¼ cup (2 fl oz/60 ml) extra-virgin olive oil

1 yellow onion, minced

4 cloves garlic, minced

3 chorizo sausages, about ¾ lb (375 g) total weight, pricked with a fork

salt and ground pepper to taste

1½ teaspoons chopped fresh flat-leaf (Italian) parsley

MAKE-AHEAD TIP: This recipe can be made up to 2 days in advance, covered, and refrigerated. Reheat over medium heat before serving.

This is one of the more substantial tapas, served mostly during the winter months when heartier fare is in order. The use of cloves and cinnamon in a savory dish is reminiscent of the cooking of North Africa, just a stone's throw away from the southern tip of Spain.

SERVES 6

❂ Pick over the chickpeas and discard any misshapen peas or stones. Rinse and drain. Place in a bowl, add cold water to cover generously, and let soak for at least 4 hours or for up to overnight.

❂ Drain the chickpeas and place in a saucepan with the cloves, cinnamon, bay leaf, thyme, and water to cover by 2 inches (5 cm). Bring to a boil over high heat, reduce the heat to low, and simmer, uncovered, until the skins just begin to crack and the chickpeas are tender, 45–60 minutes. Remove from the heat and set aside.

❂ In a large frying pan over medium heat, warm the olive oil. Add the onion, garlic, and chorizo and cook, stirring, until the onion is soft, about 10 minutes. Add the chickpeas and their liquid and simmer slowly uncovered, stirring occasionally, until the liquid is almost evaporated, about 40 minutes. Season with salt and pepper.

❂ Transfer the chorizo to a cutting board. Slice on the diagonal into slices ¼ inch (6 mm) thick. Return the chorizo slices to the pan and heat through for 1 minute.

❂ To serve, transfer the chickpeas and chorizo to a warmed serving dish. Garnish with the parsley and serve at once.

NUTRITIONAL ANALYSIS PER SERVING: Calories 594 (Kilojoules 2,495); Protein 27 g; Carbohydrates 45 g; Total Fat 35 g; Saturated Fat 10 g; Cholesterol 50 mg; Sodium 718 mg; Dietary Fiber 5 g

Catalan Mixed Grilled Vegetables

PREP TIME: 30 MINUTES

COOKING TIME: 1½ HOURS, PLUS PREPARING FIRE

INGREDIENTS

4 Asian (slender) eggplants (aubergines), 1–1¼ lb (500–625 g) total weight

5 small, ripe tomatoes

1 red bell pepper (capsicum)

1 green bell pepper (capsicum)

1 yellow onion, halved

5 tablespoons (2½ fl oz/75 ml) extra-virgin olive oil

salt and ground pepper to taste

3 tablespoons chopped fresh flat-leaf (Italian) parsley

2 cloves garlic, coarsely chopped

½ cup (2½ oz/75 g) Spanish brine-cured green olives

MAKE-AHEAD TIP: Roast the vegetables 1 day in advance. Thirty minutes before serving the dish, bring the prepared vegetables to room temperature and assemble the dish.

This tapa, known as *escalivada,* comes from the region of Catalonia in northeastern Spain. Make it in late summer, when the vegetables are at their peak.

SERVES 6

❁ Prepare a medium-hot fire in a charcoal grill. Preheat an oven to 350°F (180°C).

❁ Place the eggplants, tomatoes, bell peppers, and onion on the grill rack 4–5 inches (10–13 cm) from the fire. Grill, turning occasionally, until blackened on all sides, 8–10 minutes.

❁ Remove all the vegetables from the grill. Cut the tomatoes in half crosswise and place them, cut sides up, in a baking pan. Add the eggplants, peppers, and onion to the pan and drizzle all the vegetables with 1 tablespoon of the oil.

❁ Bake until the tomatoes collapse, about 20 minutes. Remove the pan from the oven, transfer the tomatoes to a bowl, and cover the bowl with plastic wrap. Return the remaining vegetables to the oven and bake until the eggplants and peppers collapse and are completely tender, about 30 minutes longer. Again remove the pan from the oven and transfer the peppers and eggplants to the bowl holding the tomatoes. Return the onion to the oven and continue to bake until soft, 15–20 minutes longer. Remove from the oven and transfer the onion to the bowl holding the peppers, eggplants, and tomatoes. Let stand for 15 minutes.

❁ Peel away the skins from the peppers, then discard the stems and seeds. Slice into long, narrow strips. Peel the eggplants and tear into thin strips. Slice the onion. Slip the tomatoes out of their skins and cut into quarters.

❁ Arrange the vegetables attractively on a serving platter, alternating the colors. Season with salt and pepper. Drizzle the remaining 4 tablespoons (2 fl oz/60 ml) olive oil evenly over the top. Combine the parsley and garlic on a cutting board and chop together finely. Sprinkle over the vegetables. Garnish with the olives and serve warm.

NUTRITIONAL ANALYSIS PER SERVING: Calories 173 (Kilojoules 727); Protein 2 g; Carbohydrates 14 g; Total Fat 14 g; Saturated Fat 2 g; Cholesterol 0 mg; Sodium 297 mg; Dietary Fiber 4 g

Empanaditas

PREP TIME: 1 HOUR

COOKING TIME: 45 MINUTES

INGREDIENTS

2 tablespoons olive oil

1 yellow onion, minced

2 green bell peppers (capsicums), seeded and finely chopped

3 cloves garlic, minced

¼ lb (125 g) chorizo sausages, casings removed, filling diced

½ lb (250 g) ground (minced) veal

1 cup (6 oz/185 g) peeled, seeded, and chopped tomatoes (fresh or canned)

¼ cup (1½ oz/45 g) Spanish brine-cured green olives, pitted and chopped

1 teaspoon ground cumin

large pinch of saffron threads

2 hard-boiled eggs, peeled and finely chopped

salt and ground pepper to taste

1 package (10 oz/315 g) frozen puff pastry sheets, thawed in the refrigerator

2 eggs lightly beaten with 1 tablespoon water

MAKE-AHEAD TIP: These turnovers can be formed, covered, and refrigerated up to 3 days in advance. Bake as directed. Or freeze for up to 1 month and bake them frozen, adding about 5 minutes to the baking time.

These little turnovers, made with puff pastry, can be stuffed with a variety of ingredients—peppers, wild mushrooms, greens, ground or chopped meats, chorizo, hard-boiled eggs—in nearly any combination. They can also be made larger and served with a salad as a main course.

MAKES 24 TURNOVERS; SERVES 6

❋ In a large frying pan over medium heat, warm the olive oil. Add the onion, bell peppers, and garlic and cook, stirring occasionally, until soft, about 10 minutes. Add the chorizo and veal and cook, stirring, until the veal is no longer pink, about 5 minutes. Add the tomatoes, olives, cumin, and saffron. Cover and simmer until all the ingredients are heated through, about 10 minutes. Uncover and continue to cook until the moisture evaporates, about 5 minutes. Add the hard-boiled eggs and mix well. Season with salt and pepper.

❋ Preheat an oven to 350°F (180°C).

❋ Dust a work surface and a rolling pin with flour. Roll out the puff pastry ⅛ inch (3 mm) thick. Using a round cookie cutter 3½ inches (9 cm) in diameter, cut out 24 rounds. Place about 1 tablespoon filling on one-half of each round. Brush the edges of half of the round with the egg-water mixture. Fold each round in half, enclosing the filling and forming a half-moon. Press the edges together to seal. As the turnovers are formed, arrange them on an ungreased baking sheet.

❋ Bake until golden brown, about 15 minutes. Divide the turnovers among 6 individual plates and serve hot or at room temperature.

NUTRITIONAL ANALYSIS PER SERVING: Calories 536 (Kilojoules 2,251); Protein 21 g; Carbohydrates 30 g; Total Fat 37 g; Saturated Fat 8 g; Cholesterol 189 mg; Sodium 599 mg; Dietary Fiber 2 g

Chilled Mussels with Tomatoes and Sherry Vinegar

PREP TIME: 35 MINUTES

COOKING TIME: 10 MINUTES, PLUS 2 HOURS FOR CHILLING

INGREDIENTS

1½ lb (750 g) mussels, well scrubbed and debearded

½ cup (4 fl oz/125 ml) water

2 tomatoes, peeled, seeded, and chopped

2 green (spring) onions, including tender green tops, thinly sliced

1 tablespoon chopped fresh flat-leaf (Italian) parsley

1 clove garlic, minced

½ teaspoon sweet paprika

large pinch of saffron threads

2 tablespoons extra-virgin olive oil

1 tablespoon sherry vinegar

salt and ground pepper to taste

COOKING TIP: You can make this recipe with clams instead of mussels. Increase the amount to 4 pounds (2 kg) and steam them for 3–5 minutes.

These mussels are best when served icy cold, so make the dish well in advance. Serve with plenty of crusty bread and good sherry, just as the Spanish do.

SERVES 6

⊛ Discard any mussels that fail to close to the touch. In a large frying pan over medium-high heat, bring the water to a boil. Add the mussels, cover, and cook just until most of the mussels open, 2–3 minutes. Uncover and, using tongs, transfer the opened mussels to a shallow bowl, allowing any liquid from the shells to drain back into the pan. Re-cover and continue to cook until all of the mussels have opened, 1 minute or so longer. Transfer the additional opened mussels to the bowl and discard any that failed to open. Let cool.

⊛ Meanwhile, return the pan to high heat and cook until the liquid is reduced to 2 tablespoons, about 3 minutes. Pour into a small bowl and let cool. Then add the tomatoes, green onions, parsley, garlic, paprika, saffron threads, olive oil, and vinegar. Toss to mix well. Season with salt and pepper.

⊛ When the mussels are cool, remove the top shell from each mussel and discard. Place the mussels still in their bottom shells in a serving bowl. Add the tomato mixture and toss together. Cover and refrigerate for at least 2 hours or for up to 6 hours before serving.

NUTRITIONAL ANALYSIS PER SERVING: Calories 81 (Kilojoules 340); Protein 4 g; Carbohydrates 4 g; Total Fat 6 g; Saturated Fat 1 g; Cholesterol 9 mg; Sodium 100 mg; Dietary Fiber 1 g

Shrimp and Saffron Pancakes

PREP TIME: 35 MINUTES, PLUS 1 HOUR FOR RESTING

COOKING TIME: 25 MINUTES

INGREDIENTS

2 tablespoons olive oil, plus oil for frying

¼ cup (¾ oz/20 g) minced green (spring) onion, including tender green tops

¾ cup (4 oz/125 g) all-purpose (plain) flour

½ cup (2 oz/60 g) chickpea (garbanzo bean) flour

½ teaspoon baking powder

½ teaspoon salt

½ teaspoon ground pepper

½ lb (250 g) small shrimp (prawns), peeled and finely chopped

3 tablespoons chopped fresh flat-leaf (Italian) parsley, plus sprigs for garnish (optional)

½ teaspoon sweet paprika

large pinch of saffron threads

1½ cups (12 fl oz/375 ml) water

SERVING TIP: Serve these pancakes as they do in Andalusia, with a glass of golden amontillado sherry.

In Andalusia, in southern Spain, flamenco dancing, galloping horses, and the very best array of tapas are commonplace. These simple little Andalusian pancakes are typically made with shrimp the size of a small thumbnail, a specialty of the region. Use the smallest shrimp you can find. Chickpea flour is available at well-stocked health-food stores.

MAKES ABOUT 20 PANCAKES; SERVES 6

❊ In a small frying pan over low heat, warm the 2 tablespoons olive oil. Add the green onion, cover, and cook until soft, about 3 minutes. Remove from the heat and let cool slightly.

❊ In a bowl, stir together the all-purpose flour, chickpea flour, baking powder, salt, and pepper. Add the shrimp, cooked green onion, chopped parsley, paprika, saffron, and water. Stir well. The batter should be the consistency of very heavy (double) cream. Cover and let stand at room temperature for 1 hour or refrigerate for up to overnight.

❊ In a large frying pan, pour in olive oil to a depth of ¼ inch (6 mm) and place over medium-high heat. When the oil is hot, drop in 2 tablespoons batter for each pancake, spreading out each mound with the back of a spoon to form a cake about 2½ inches (6 cm) in diameter. Do not crowd the pan. Fry, turning once, until golden, about 2 minutes on each side. Using a slotted spatula, transfer to paper towels to drain. Keep warm. Fry the remaining batter in the same way.

❊ Arrange on a warmed platter and serve at once. Garnish with parsley sprigs, if desired.

NUTRITIONAL ANALYSIS PER SERVING: Calories 238 (Kilojoules 1,000); Protein 10 g; Carbohydrates 21 g; Total Fat 13 g; Saturated Fat 2 g; Cholesterol 47 mg; Sodium 283 mg; Dietary Fiber 1 g

Fava Beans with Pecorino, Olive Oil, and Lemon

PREP TIME: 45 MINUTES

COOKING TIME: 5 MINUTES

INGREDIENTS

4 lb (2 kg) fresh fava (broad) beans, shelled

3 tablespoons extra-virgin olive oil

2 tablespoons lemon juice

1 clove garlic, minced

1 tablespoon chopped fresh flat-leaf (Italian) parsley

½ teaspoon grated lemon zest

salt and ground pepper to taste

wedge of pecorino cheese, about 3 oz (90 g)

6 lemon wedges

MAKE-AHEAD TIP: The fava beans can be peeled 1 day in advance, covered, and refrigerated. To serve the salad, bring the fava beans to room temperature.

Peeling a batch of fava beans can seem like a daunting task, but the process is actually quite simple and the results are well worth the time. Try to find young, tender spring favas for this delicious salad.

SERVES 6

❁ Bring a large pot three-fourths full of water to a boil over high heat. Add the shelled fava beans, reduce the heat to medium, and simmer until the skins begin to soften, about 20 seconds. Drain and let cool.

❁ To peel the beans, using a small knife, pierce the skin of each bean opposite the end where it was attached to the pod. The bean will slip easily from its skin. Discard the skins and set the beans aside.

❁ In a bowl, whisk together the olive oil, lemon juice, garlic, parsley, and lemon zest. Season with salt and pepper. Add the fava beans and toss together. Using a vegetable peeler, cut the pecorino into thin shavings directly over the bowl. Toss the mixture gently.

❁ Transfer to a platter and garnish with the lemon wedges. Serve immediately.

NUTRITIONAL ANALYSIS PER SERVING: Calories 196 (Kilojoules 823); Protein 12 g; Carbohydrates 14 g; Total Fat 12 g; Saturated Fat 4 g; Cholesterol 14 mg; Sodium 223 mg; Dietary Fiber 4 g

Warm Shrimp Salad with Salsa Verde

PREP TIME: 45 MINUTES

COOKING TIME: 5 MINUTES

INGREDIENTS

FOR THE SAUCE

⅓ cup (½ oz/15 g) chopped fresh flat-leaf (Italian) parsley

2 tablespoons chopped fresh chives

½ teaspoon chopped fresh thyme

¼ teaspoon chopped fresh oregano

¼ cup (2 oz/60 g) capers, chopped

2 cloves garlic, minced

¼ cup (2 fl oz/60 ml) lemon juice

⅓ cup (3 fl oz/80 ml) extra-virgin olive oil

salt and ground pepper to taste

½ cup (4 fl oz/125 ml) bottled clam juice or water

1¼ lb (625 g) shrimp (prawns)

6 lemon wedges

fresh chives

6 crusty wheat rolls, toasted and split

1 clove garlic

MAKE-AHEAD TIP: The shrimp can be cooked up to 1 day in advance, covered, and refrigerated. Bring to room temperature before serving.

This brightly flavored salsa verde is a perfect dressing for warm poached shrimp. As an alternative to shrimp, substitute 2 pounds (1 kg) mussels, 3 pounds (1.5 kg) clams, or 1¼ pounds (625 g) firm-fleshed fish fillets such as tuna or halibut. The mussels will cook in 2–3 minutes, the clams in 3–5 minutes, and the fillets in 7–10 minutes (for a piece 1 inch/2.5 cm thick). Serve with a first-rate Soave.

SERVES 6

❁ To make the sauce, in a bowl, stir together the parsley, chives, thyme, oregano, capers, minced garlic, lemon juice, and olive oil. Season with salt and pepper and set aside.

❁ In a frying pan over medium heat, bring the clam juice or water to a boil. Add the shrimp, cover, and cook until they turn pink and begin to curl, 1–2 minutes. Using a slotted spoon, transfer the shrimp to a plate.

❁ Raise the heat to high and boil the juices until reduced to 1–2 tablespoons, 1–2 minutes. Remove from the heat, let cool, then stir into the sauce.

❁ As soon as the shrimp are cool enough to handle, peel them, discarding the shells, then devein. Add to the sauce and toss to coat evenly.

❁ Place the shrimp on a platter and garnish with the lemon wedges and chives. Rub the warm toasted rolls lightly with the whole garlic clove and serve immediately with the shrimp.

NUTRITIONAL ANALYSIS PER SERVING: Calories 366 (Kilojoules 1,537); Protein 22 g; Carbohydrates 34 g; Total Fat 16 g; Saturated Fat 2 g; Cholesterol 116 mg; Sodium 726 mg; Dietary Fiber 1 g

Mozzarella in Carrozza

PREP TIME: 20 MINUTES

COOKING TIME: 15 MINUTES

INGREDIENTS

5 eggs

3 tablespoons milk

1 teaspoon salt

½ loaf coarse country bread, about ½ lb (250 g), cut into slices ½ inch (12 mm) thick

1 lb (500 g) fresh mozzarella cheese, cut into slices ¼ inch (6 mm) thick

olive oil for frying

Cut into strips, this Italian cheese sandwich makes a terrific antipasto. In Naples, it is usually deep-fried, but shallow frying is the preferred method because less oil is absorbed. Serve as soon as possible after cooking to prevent the strips from becoming soggy. If you like, slip some chopped olives, a pinch of red pepper flakes, or some sun-dried tomatoes between the bread slices along with the cheese. Serve with a glass of crisp and fruity Pinot Grigio.

MAKES ABOUT 24 PIECES; SERVES 6

❀ In a large, shallow bowl, beat together the eggs, milk, and salt until blended.

❀ Using 2 slices of bread and 1 slice of cheese for each, make as many cheese sandwiches as you can. One at a time, dip the sandwiches into the egg mixture, coating evenly.

❀ In a deep, heavy frying pan over medium-high heat, pour in olive oil to a depth of ¼ inch (6 mm) and warm over medium-high heat just until it begins to ripple. In batches, place the sandwiches in the hot oil in a single layer and cook, pressing down on the tops with a spatula and turning once, until golden, about 1 minute on each side. Using a slotted spatula or tongs, transfer to paper towels to drain. Keep warm until all the sandwiches are cooked.

❀ Cut the sandwiches into strips 1 inch (2.5 cm) wide and arrange on a platter. Serve immediately.

NUTRITIONAL ANALYSIS PER SERVING: Calories 424 (Kilojoules 1,781); Protein 22 g; Carbohydrates 23 g; Total Fat 26 g; Saturated Fat 2 g; Cholesterol 232 mg; Sodium 728 mg; Dietary Fiber 1 g

Roasted Peppers with Anchovies and Olives

PREP TIME: 30 MINUTES

COOKING TIME: 10 MINUTES

INGREDIENTS

4 large red bell peppers (capsicums)

4 large yellow bell peppers (capsicums)

2 tablespoons extra-virgin olive oil

1 tablespoon balsamic vinegar

salt and ground pepper to taste

6 anchovy fillets

⅓ cup (2 oz/60 g) Kalamata or Niçoise olives

2 tablespoons chopped fresh flat-leaf (Italian) parsley

1 clove garlic, chopped

MAKE-AHEAD TIP: The peppers can be roasted up to 3 days in advance, covered, and refrigerated. Bring to room temperature before continuing with the recipe.

This dish pairs well with Bruschetta with Tomatoes and Basil (page 66). If you like, garnish the roasted peppers with ¼ cup (2 oz/60 g) capers or caperberries.

SERVES 6

❁ Preheat a broiler (griller).

❁ Cut the bell peppers in half lengthwise. Remove and discard the stems, seeds, and ribs. Place, cut sides down, on a baking sheet. Broil (grill) until the skins blacken and blister. Remove from the broiler, drape the peppers loosely with aluminum foil, and let cool for 10 minutes, then peel away the skins. Cut the peppers lengthwise into strips 1 inch (2.5 cm) wide.

❁ In a bowl, combine the pepper strips, olive oil, and vinegar and stir together. Season with salt and pepper. Set aside.

❁ Place the anchovy fillets in a bowl, add cold water just to cover, and let soak for 10 minutes. Remove from the water and pat dry with paper towels.

❁ Arrange the peppers on a platter with the anchovies and olives. Combine the parsley and garlic on a cutting board and chop together finely. Sprinkle over the peppers and serve.

NUTRITIONAL ANALYSIS PER SERVING: Calories 114 (Kilojoules 479); Protein 2 g; Carbohydrates 10 g; Total Fat 8 g; Saturated Fat 1 g; Cholesterol 2 mg; Sodium 320 mg; Dietary Fiber 2 g

Panzanella

PREP TIME: 20 MINUTES, PLUS 1 HOUR FOR CHILLING

INGREDIENTS

½ lb (250 g) 2- to 3-day-old coarse country bread

½ cup (4 fl oz/125 ml) cold water

6 ripe tomatoes, peeled, seeded, and coarsely diced (about ¾ cup/ 6 oz/185 g)

1 red (Spanish) onion, thinly sliced

1 English (hothouse) cucumber, peeled, seeded, and diced

2 tablespoons capers

½ cup (½ oz/15 g) fresh basil leaves

2 tablespoons red wine vinegar

¼ cup (2 fl oz/60 ml) balsamic vinegar

¼ cup (2 fl oz/60 ml) extra-virgin olive oil

salt and ground pepper to taste

SERVING TIP: This salad is best served the same day you make it.

Here is an ingenious way to use up stale bread. The success of the recipe depends upon the type of bread you use. It must have a dense, coarse texture, rather than a light, cottony one. Full-flavored sun-ripened tomatoes are equally important to the final result.

SERVES 6

❀ Cut the bread into slices 1 inch (2.5 cm) thick. Place in a shallow bowl in a single layer and sprinkle with the water. Let stand for 1 minute. Carefully squeeze the water from the bread. Tear the bread into rough 1-inch (2.5-cm) chunks and place them on paper towels for 10 minutes to absorb excess moisture.

❀ In a bowl, combine the tomatoes, onion, cucumber, and capers. Tear the basil leaves into small pieces and add to the mixture. Add the bread and toss carefully to avoid breaking up the bread too much.

❀ In a small bowl, whisk together the red wine vinegar, balsamic vinegar, and olive oil. Season with salt and pepper. Drizzle over the bread-tomato mixture and toss gently to mix. Cover and refrigerate for 1 hour.

❀ Transfer to individual bowls and serve at once.

NUTRITIONAL ANALYSIS PER SERVING: Calories 213 (Kilojoules 895); Protein 4 g; Carbohydrates 26 g; Total Fat 11 g; Saturated Fat 2 g; Cholesterol 0 mg; Sodium 366 mg; Dietary Fiber 2 g

Focaccia with Gorgonzola, Pine Nuts, and Green Onions

PREP TIME: 35 MINUTES, PLUS 2½ HOURS FOR STANDING AND RISING

COOKING TIME: 25 MINUTES, PLUS 30 MINUTES FOR HEATING STONE

INGREDIENTS

FOR THE DOUGH

2 teaspoons active dry yeast

¼ cup (2 fl oz/60 ml) warm water (115°F/46°C)

2 cups (10 oz/315 g) all-purpose (plain) or bread (hard-wheat) flour

½ teaspoon salt

⅔ cup (5 fl oz/160 ml) cold water

1 tablespoon extra-virgin olive oil

FOR THE TOPPING

¼ cup (1¼ oz/37 g) pine nuts

¼ lb (125 g) Gorgonzola cheese, at room temperature, crumbled

2 oz (60 g) fontina cheese, shredded

3 green (spring) onions, including tender green tops, thinly sliced

Gorgonzola, a blue-veined cow's milk cheese from northern Italy, melts beautifully onto the top of this flat bread.

MAKES TWO 7-INCH (18-CM) ROUNDS; SERVES 6

❁ To make the dough, in a bowl, using a wooden spoon, stir together the yeast, warm water, and ¼ cup (1½ oz/45 g) of the flour. Let stand until foamy, about 20 minutes. Add the remaining 1¾ cups (8½ fl oz/270 g) flour, the salt, cold water, and olive oil. Stir with the wooden spoon until the dough pulls away from the sides of the bowl. Turn out the dough onto a well-floured work surface and knead until soft, supple, and smooth yet still moist, 7–10 minutes. Place the dough in an oiled bowl, turning it once to coat with oil. Cover the bowl with plastic wrap, transfer to a warm place (about 75°F/24°C), and let the dough rise until doubled in bulk, 1–2 hours.

❁ Meanwhile, make the topping: In a small, dry frying pan over medium heat, toast the pine nuts, stirring constantly, until golden, about 1 minute. Remove from the heat, pour into a bowl, and let cool. When cool, add the Gorgonzola, fontina, and green onions. Toss to mix well.

❁ About 45 minutes before serving, place a pizza stone or baking tiles on the bottom rack of an oven and preheat to 500°F (260°C).

❁ On a floured work surface, punch down the dough and divide in half. Shape each half into a smooth ball. Roll out 1 ball into a round 7 inches (18 cm) in diameter and ½ inch (12 mm) thick. Transfer the dough to a well-floured pizza peel or a rimless baking sheet. Scatter half of the cheese mixture evenly over the surface to within ½ inch (12 mm) of the edge.

❁ Slide the dough round onto the heated stone or tiles and bake until golden and crisp, 10–12 minutes. Carefully slip the peel or baking sheet under the focaccia and transfer to a cutting board. Repeat with the remaining dough and cheese mixture.

❁ While the second round is baking, cut the first focaccia into 6 wedges and serve.

NUTRITIONAL ANALYSIS PER SERVING: Calories 358 (Kilojoules 1,504); Protein 14 g; Carbohydrates 42 g; Total Fat 16 g; Saturated Fat 7 g; Cholesterol 28 mg; Sodium 630 mg; Dietary Fiber 3 g

Caponata

PREP TIME: 40 MINUTES, PLUS 30 MINUTES FOR DRAINING EGGPLANT

COOKING TIME: 50 MINUTES, PLUS 1 HOUR FOR COOLING

INGREDIENTS

3 tablespoons pine nuts

1 eggplant (aubergine), about 1 lb (500 g)

coarse salt for eggplant

4 tablespoons (2 fl oz/60 ml) extra-virgin olive oil

1 small yellow onion, diced

1 small red bell pepper (capsicum), seeded and diced

1 celery stalk, diced

3 cups (18 oz/560 g) peeled, seeded, and chopped tomatoes (fresh or canned)

½ cup (2½ oz/75 g) brine-cured green olives, pitted and coarsely chopped

2 tablespoons capers

2 tablespoons red wine vinegar

2 tablespoons tomato paste

½ teaspoon sugar

table salt and ground pepper to taste

MAKE-AHEAD TIP: This recipe can be completed up to 2 days in advance, covered, and refrigerated. Bring to room temperature before serving.

Sicily is known for its excellent eggplants, and Sicilians use them liberally in this famous sweet-and-sour antipasto. Serve at room temperature just as it is or as a topping for grilled bread. A robust red wine pairs well with this highly seasoned dish.

SERVES 6

❀ In a small, dry frying pan over medium heat, toast the pine nuts, stirring constantly, until golden and fragrant, about 1 minute. Transfer to a plate and set aside.

❀ Cut the eggplant into ½-inch (12-mm) cubes. Place in a colander, sprinkling each layer with coarse salt. Let stand for 30 minutes to drain off the bitter juices.

❀ Preheat an oven to 375°F (190°C).

❀ Rinse the eggplant and pat dry with paper towels. Place on a baking sheet, drizzle with 2 tablespoons of the olive oil, and toss to coat. Spread evenly in a single layer on the baking sheet. Bake, tossing occasionally, until lightly golden, 15–20 minutes. Remove from the oven and set aside.

❀ Meanwhile, in a large frying pan over medium heat, warm the remaining 2 tablespoons olive oil. Add the onion, bell pepper, and celery, stir well, cover, and cook until soft, 8–10 minutes. Uncover and cook, stirring occasionally, until the vegetables start to turn golden brown, 6–8 minutes.

❀ Add the tomatoes, olives, capers, vinegar, tomato paste, and sugar and cook until the liquid evaporates, 20–30 minutes. Add the eggplant and pine nuts and stir well. Season with table salt and pepper.

❀ Transfer to a serving bowl and let cool to room temperature before serving.

NUTRITIONAL ANALYSIS PER SERVING: Calories 173 (Kilojoules 727); Protein 3 g; Carbohydrates 14 g; Total Fat 14 g; Saturated Fat 2 g; Cholesterol 0 mg; Sodium 531 mg; Dietary Fiber 4 g

Fennel Frittata

PREP TIME: 30 MINUTES

COOKING TIME: 35 MINUTES

INGREDIENTS

2 small fennel bulbs

2 tablespoons olive oil

2 cloves garlic, minced

½ teaspoon grated lemon zest

1 tablespoon lemon juice

salt and ground pepper to taste

8 eggs

3 tablespoons milk

½ cup (2 oz/60 g) grated pecorino or Parmesan cheese

2 tablespoons chopped fresh flat-leaf (Italian) parsley

MAKE-AHEAD TIP: The frittata can be cooked up to 1 day in advance, covered, and refrigerated. Bring to room temperature before serving.

Other vegetables such as roasted bell peppers (capsicums), sautéed zucchini (courgettes), or caramelized onions can be used instead of the fennel. Frittatas are traditionally served as antipasti, but they also make a good light main course.

SERVES 6

❂ Cut off the stems and feathery tops and any bruised outer stalks from the fennel bulbs. Dice the bulbs.

❂ Preheat an oven to 400°F (200°C).

❂ In a large frying pan over medium-low heat, warm 1 tablespoon of the olive oil. Add the fennel and cook, stirring occasionally, until almost soft, 12–15 minutes. Add the garlic, lemon zest, and lemon juice and stir together. Continue to cook, stirring, until the fennel is very soft, about 5 minutes. Season with salt and pepper. Remove from the heat and let cool slightly.

❂ In a bowl, whisk together the eggs, milk, cheese, and parsley until frothy. Add the fennel and mix well. Season with salt and pepper.

❂ In a 10-inch (25-cm) nonstick ovenproof frying pan over medium-high heat, warm the remaining 1 tablespoon olive oil. Add the egg mixture, reduce the heat to medium, and cook, occasionally loosening the edges with a spatula to allow the uncooked portion to run underneath, until the bottom of the frittata is set and the top is still runny, 7–8 minutes. Transfer to the oven and continue to cook until the eggs are set and the top is golden brown, 6–7 minutes.

❂ Remove the frittata from the oven and loosen the bottom with a spatula. Invert a plate over the top of the frying pan. Holding them together firmly, flip the plate and pan so the frittata falls onto the plate.

❂ Cut the frittata into wedges and serve hot, warm, or at room temperature.

NUTRITIONAL ANALYSIS PER SERVING: Calories 195 (Kilojoules 819); Protein 13 g; Carbohydrates 4 g; Total Fat 14 g; Saturated Fat 5 g; Cholesterol 294 mg; Sodium 270 mg; Dietary Fiber 1 g

Bite-Sized Rice Croquettes

PREP TIME: 40 MINUTES, PLUS 1 HOUR FOR COOLING

COOKING TIME: 40 MINUTES

INGREDIENTS

2 tablespoons extra-virgin olive oil

½ small yellow onion, minced

1 cup (7 oz/220 g) Arborio rice

1¼ cups (10 fl oz/310 ml) chicken broth

1¼ cups (10 fl oz/310 ml) milk

⅔ cup (5 oz/150 g) black olive paste *(see page 110)*

salt and ground pepper to taste

¼ cup (1 oz/30 g) grated Parmesan cheese

1 cup (5 oz/155 g) all-purpose (plain) flour

4 eggs

½ cup (4 fl oz/125 ml) water

4 cups (1 lb/500 g) fine dried bread crumbs

vegetable oil and olive oil for deep-frying

MAKE-AHEAD TIP: The croquettes can be prepared up to 3 days in advance, covered, and refrigerated. Deep-fry just before serving.

These tiny croquettes are a specialty of northern Italy. Crispy on the outside and creamy inside, they are perfect accompanied with a glass of ruby red Barolo.

MAKES 60 CROQUETTES; SERVES 12

❀ In a saucepan over medium heat, warm the olive oil. Add the onion and cook, stirring occasionally, until soft, about 7 minutes. Add the rice and continue to cook, stirring constantly, until coated with oil and hot, about 2 minutes.

❀ Meanwhile, in a saucepan over medium heat, combine the broth and milk and bring just to a simmer. Immediately add the milk-broth mixture to the rice with ⅓ cup (2½ oz/75 g) of the olive paste and the salt and pepper. Bring to a simmer, reduce the heat to low, cover, and cook slowly until all the liquid has been absorbed and the rice is tender, about 20 minutes. Stir in the remaining ⅓ cup (2½ oz/75 g) olive paste and the cheese. Remove from the heat and let cool completely, about 1 hour.

❀ Using a scant tablespoon of the rice mixture for each croquette, form the mixture into balls the size of large olives, about 1 inch (2.5 cm) in diameter. Place the flour in a shallow bowl. In another bowl, whisk together the eggs and water until blended. Place the bread crumbs in a third bowl. Roll the rice balls in the flour, then in the egg, and finally in the bread crumbs, coating evenly each time. As the balls are coated, place on a baking sheet.

❀ In a deep frying pan or a saucepan, pour in equal parts vegetable oil and olive oil to a depth of 1 inch (2.5 cm) and heat to 375°F (190°C) on a deep-frying thermometer. Add the balls, in batches, and fry, turning as needed, until golden on all sides, 1–1½ minutes. Using a slotted spoon, transfer to a wire rack placed over a paper towel–lined tray to drain. Keep warm until all of the balls are cooked.

❀ Arrange on a platter and serve immediately.

NUTRITIONAL ANALYSIS PER SERVING: Calories 414 (Kilojoules 1,739); Protein 11 g; Carbohydrates 50 g; Total Fat 19 g; Saturated Fat 4 g; Cholesterol 76 mg; Sodium 570 mg; Dietary Fiber 3 g

Crostini with Sweet-and-Sour Chicken Livers

PREP TIME: 20 MINUTES

COOKING TIME: 25 MINUTES

INGREDIENTS

3 tablespoons extra-virgin olive oil

2 oz (60 g) pancetta, finely chopped

¼ cup (1½ oz/45 g) finely chopped yellow onion

1 teaspoon chopped fresh sage, plus small whole leaves for garnish (optional)

2 tablespoons dry Marsala or dry white wine

½ lb (250 g) chicken livers, trimmed of fat and sinew

salt and ground pepper to taste

1 clove garlic, minced

1 tablespoon capers, chopped

1 tablespoon balsamic vinegar

12 slices coarse country bread, each about 3 inches (7.5 cm) in diameter and ¼ inch (6 mm) thick

COOKING TIP: You can use duck livers in place of the chicken livers.

Crostini are simply toasted slices of bread. In Italy, they are used as a base for everything from wilted greens and white beans to Gorgonzola, prosciutto, salt cod, and *fegatini agrodolce*, sweet-and-sour chicken livers. Serve this Tuscan specialty with a glass of full-bodied Chianti.

SERVES 6

❁ In a frying pan over medium heat, warm 1 tablespoon of the olive oil. Add the pancetta and sauté until golden and the fat is rendered, about 5 minutes. Add the onion and chopped sage and cook, stirring occasionally, until the onion is soft, about 10 minutes. Add the Marsala or white wine and simmer until it evaporates, 2–3 minutes. Transfer the mixture to a cutting board and mince. Place in a bowl and set aside.

❁ In the same pan over low heat, warm the remaining 2 tablespoons olive oil. Place the livers in the pan in a single layer and cook until they start to turn golden, 2–3 minutes. Turn the livers over and continue to cook until firm to the touch yet still pink on the inside, 2–3 minutes longer. Season with salt and pepper. Transfer to a cutting board and let cool for 15 minutes.

❁ Preheat a broiler (griller).

❁ When the livers are cool, chop coarsely and add to the bowl with the pancetta mixture. Add the garlic, capers, and balsamic vinegar. Season with salt and pepper.

❁ Arrange the bread slices on a baking sheet, slip under the broiler (griller), and toast, turning once, until golden, 30–60 seconds on each side.

❁ Spread the liver mixture on the warm bread slices. Arrange on a platter, garnish with sage leaves, if using, and serve immediately.

NUTRITIONAL ANALYSIS PER SERVING: Calories 214 (Kilojoules 899); Protein 11 g; Carbohydrates 18 g; Total Fat 10 g; Saturated Fat 2 g; Cholesterol 172 mg; Sodium 376 mg; Dietary Fiber 1 g

Crispy Polenta Fingers with Tomato-Pepper Sauce

PREP TIME: 30 MINUTES, PLUS 2 HOURS FOR CHILLING

COOKING TIME: 40 MINUTES

INGREDIENTS

3 cups (24 fl oz/750 ml) water

½ teaspoon coarse salt, plus salt to taste

½ cup (3 oz/90 g) plus 2 tablespoons polenta

3 tablespoons grated Parmesan cheese

1 tablespoon unsalted butter, at room temperature

1 teaspoon chopped fresh rosemary

ground black pepper to taste

FOR THE SAUCE

1 large red bell pepper (capsicum)

2 tablespoons sour cream

1 tablespoon tomato paste

½ cup (4 fl oz/125 ml) heavy (double) cream

1 teaspoon balsamic vinegar

pinch of cayenne pepper

salt and ground black pepper to taste

1½ cups (7½ oz/235 g) all-purpose (plain) flour

olive oil and safflower oil for deep-frying

SERVES 6–8

❁ Butter a 5-by-9-inch (13-by-23-cm) loaf pan. In a saucepan over high heat, bring the water to a boil. Add the ½ teaspoon salt, reduce the heat to medium, and slowly add the polenta, whisking constantly. Continue to whisk the mixture until it thickens, about 2 minutes. Change to a wooden spoon and continue to simmer, stirring periodically, until it pulls away from the sides of the pan and the spoon stands upright, unaided, in the polenta, 20–25 minutes. Add the cheese, butter, and rosemary and stir to mix well. Remove from the heat, season with salt and pepper, and pour into the prepared pan. Smooth the top with a rubber spatula, cover, and refrigerate until set, about 2 hours.

❁ Meanwhile, make the sauce: Preheat a broiler (griller). Cut the bell pepper in half lengthwise. Remove and discard the stem, seeds, and ribs. Place, cut sides down, on a baking sheet. Broil (grill) until the skins blacken and blister. Remove from the broiler, drape the pepper halves loosely with aluminum foil, and let cool for 10 minutes, then peel away the skin.

❁ Place the roasted pepper in a blender along with the sour cream and tomato paste and blend until a smooth paste forms. Transfer to a bowl and add the heavy cream, vinegar, and cayenne. Whisk until the cream thickens slightly. Season with salt and black pepper. Cover and refrigerate until serving.

❁ Run a knife around the polenta to loosen it from the pan. Invert the pan to unmold the polenta. Cut into slices ½ inch (12 mm) thick. Cut the slices into sticks 3 inches (7.5 cm) long by ½ inch (12 mm) wide. You should have about 30 sticks. Place the flour in a bowl and, in batches, dust the sticks lightly with the flour. In a large, deep frying pan or in a saucepan over medium-high heat, pour in equal parts olive oil and safflower oil to a depth of 1 inch (2.5 cm) and heat to 375°F (190°C) on a deep-frying thermometer. Add the polenta sticks, in batches, and fry, turning as needed, until golden on all sides, 1–2 minutes. Using a slotted spoon, transfer to paper towels to drain. Sprinkle with salt. Keep warm until all the sticks are cooked.

❁ Serve warm with the sauce.

NUTRITIONAL ANALYSIS PER SERVING: Calories 404 (Kilojoules 1,697); Protein 7 g; Carbohydrates 44 g; Total Fat 22 g; Saturated Fat 8 g; Cholesterol 33 mg; Sodium 169 mg; Dietary Fiber 4 g

Bruschetta with Tomatoes and Basil

PREP TIME: 15 MINUTES

COOKING TIME: 5 MINUTES, PLUS PREPARING FIRE

INGREDIENTS

6 slices coarse country bread, each about ⅜ inch (1 cm) thick

2 cloves garlic

¼ cup (2 fl oz/60 ml) good-quality extra-virgin olive oil

12 thin tomato slices

coarse salt

6 fresh basil leaves

SERVING TIP: Serve the bruschetta with cured black olives that have been warmed in a pan with rosemary and thyme sprigs, bay leaves, and a pinch of red pepper flakes.

Bruschetta—thick slices of rustic bread grilled over an open fire, rubbed with garlic, brushed with green-gold olive oil, and maybe sprinkled with a little coarse salt—celebrates the olive harvest. Here, tomatoes and basil have been added to the classic recipe. Serve this antipasto at the height of summer when the tomatoes from your garden or the local farmers' market are at their prime and the basil is tender and sweet. Although a broiler (griller) or toaster can be used, a charcoal fire imparts the best flavor.

SERVES 6

❀ Prepare a medium-hot fire in a charcoal grill.

❀ Place the bread slices on the grill rack 4–5 inches (10–13 cm) from the fire and grill, turning once, until golden on each side, 30–60 seconds.

❀ Transfer the bread to a work surface and, while still warm, rub the slices lightly on both sides with a garlic clove, handling the toasted bread as if it were a grater. Place the olive oil in a small bowl, and brush each bread slice on one side with some of the oil. Top each slice with 2 tomato slices. Sprinkle the tomato slices with coarse salt. Stack the basil leaves on top of one another, roll up, and slice into thin ribbons. Garnish the tomatoes with the basil.

❀ Arrange on a platter and serve immediately.

NUTRITIONAL ANALYSIS PER SERVING: Calories 136 (Kilojoules 572); Protein 2 g; Carbohydrates 11 g; Total Fat 10 g; Saturated Fat 1 g; Cholesterol 0 mg; Sodium 116 mg; Dietary Fiber 1 g

White Bean Salad with Red, Green, and Yellow Peppers

PREP TIME: 30 MINUTES, PLUS 4 HOURS FOR SOAKING AND 1 HOUR FOR COOLING

COOKING TIME: 40 MINUTES

INGREDIENTS

1 cup (7 oz/220 g) dried cannellini beans

6 tablespoons (3 fl oz/90 ml) extra-virgin olive oil

5 tablespoons (2½ fl oz/75 ml) red wine vinegar, or as needed

salt and ground pepper to taste

1 red bell pepper (capsicum), seeded and cut into ¼-inch (6-mm) dice

1 green bell pepper (capsicum), seeded and cut into ¼-inch (6-mm) dice

1 yellow bell pepper (capsicum), seeded and cut into ¼-inch (6-mm) dice

1 small red (Spanish) onion, cut into ¼-inch (6-mm) dice

1 clove garlic, minced

1 tablespoon chopped fresh oregano, plus small sprigs for garnish

COOKING TIP: If you like, add 5 ounces (155 g) goat cheese, crumbled, along with the bell pepper and onion.

Tuscans love beans, especially cannellini beans. In some cases, they cook them with garlic and plenty of Tuscany's golden olive oil and eat them warm. They make them into salads, too, such as this colorful antipasto, which is also ideal for toting to a picnic lunch.

SERVES 6

❀ Pick over the beans and discard any misshapen beans or stones. Rinse the beans and drain. Place in a bowl, add plenty of cold water to cover, and let soak for 4 hours or for up to overnight. Drain and place in a saucepan with water to cover by 4 inches (10 cm). Bring to a boil over high heat, reduce the heat to low, and simmer, uncovered, until the skins just begin to crack and the beans are tender, 30–40 minutes. Remove from the heat, drain, and transfer to a bowl.

❀ While the beans are cooking, in a small bowl, whisk together the olive oil and the 5 tablespoons (2½ fl oz/75 ml) vinegar to form a dressing. Season with salt and pepper.

❀ Add the dressing to the warm beans and let stand until the beans are cool, about 1 hour.

❀ Add the bell peppers, onion, garlic, and chopped oregano to the beans and mix well. Taste and add more salt, pepper, and vinegar, as needed.

❀ To serve, transfer to a serving bowl and garnish with oregano sprigs.

NUTRITIONAL ANALYSIS PER SERVING: Calories 251 (Kilojoules 1,054); Protein 8 g; Carbohydrates 25 g; Total Fat 14 g; Saturated Fat 2 g; Cholesterol 0 mg; Sodium 11 mg; Dietary Fiber 4 g

Pizzetta with Tomatoes and Mozzarella

PREP TIME: 40 MINUTES, PLUS 2½ HOURS FOR STANDING AND RISING

COOKING TIME: 50 MINUTES, PLUS 30 MINUTES FOR HEATING STONE

INGREDIENTS

FOR THE DOUGH

1½ teaspoons active dry yeast

3 tablespoons warm water (115°F/46°C)

3 tablespoons plus 1¼ cups (6½ oz/200 g) all-purpose (plain) or bread (hard-wheat) flour

¼ teaspoon salt

½ cup (4 fl oz/125 ml) cold water

1 tablespoon milk

1 tablespoon extra-virgin olive oil

2 cups (12 oz/375 g) peeled, seeded, and chopped tomatoes (fresh or canned)

salt and ground pepper to taste

¼ lb (125 g) fresh mozzarella cheese, coarsely shredded

MAKE-AHEAD TIP: You can make the dough a day in advance and let it rise overnight in the refrigerator. Bring to room temperature before shaping.

A pizzetta is simply a miniature pizza, here topped with tomatoes and fresh mozzarella. If you are short of time, substitute 1 pound (500 g) store-bought pizza dough for the homemade.

MAKES TWO 7-INCH (18-CM) ROUNDS; SERVES 6

❋ To make the dough, in a bowl, using a wooden spoon, stir together the yeast, warm water, and the 3 tablespoons flour. Let stand until foamy, about 20 minutes. Add the 1¼ cups (6½ oz/200 g) flour, salt, cold water, milk, and olive oil. Stir with the wooden spoon until the dough pulls away from the sides of the bowl. Turn out the dough onto a floured work surface and knead until soft, supple, and smooth yet still moist, 7–10 minutes. Place the dough in an oiled bowl, turning it once to coat with oil. Cover the bowl with plastic wrap, transfer to a warm place (about 75°F/24°C), and let the dough rise until doubled in bulk, 1–2 hours.

❋ Meanwhile, in a nonstick frying pan over medium-high heat, bring the tomatoes to a boil. Reduce the heat to low and simmer until the tomatoes are very thick and the consistency of tomato paste, 30–40 minutes. Remove from the heat, season with salt and pepper, and let cool.

❋ About 45 minutes before serving, place a pizza stone or baking tiles on the bottom rack of an oven and preheat to 500°F (260°C).

❋ On a floured surface, punch down the dough and divide in half. Shape each half into a smooth ball. Roll out 1 ball into a round 7 inches (18 cm) in diameter and ¼ inch (6 mm) thick. Transfer the round to a well-floured pizza peel or a rimless baking sheet. Spread half of the tomatoes over the surface to within ½ inch (12 mm) of the edge. Sprinkle evenly with half of the cheese.

❋ Slide the dough round onto the heated stone or tiles and bake until golden brown and crisp on the bottom, 8–10 minutes. Carefully slip the peel or baking sheet under the pizzetta and transfer to a cutting board. Repeat with the remaining dough and topping ingredients.

❋ While the second pizzetta is baking, cut the first pizzetta into 6 wedges and serve.

NUTRITIONAL ANALYSIS PER SERVING: Calories 246 (Kilojoules 1,033); Protein 9 g; Carbohydrates 35 g; Total Fat 8 g; Saturated Fat 1 g; Cholesterol 14 mg; Sodium 116 mg; Dietary Fiber 2 g

Spinach Tiropites

PREP TIME: 1 HOUR

COOKING TIME: 20 MINUTES

INGREDIENTS

1½ lb (750 g) spinach, tough stems removed and coarsely chopped

1½ cups (7½ oz/235 g) crumbled feta cheese

½ cup (2 oz/60 g) grated kefalotiri, Parmesan, or pecorino cheese

4 eggs, lightly beaten

2 tablespoons chopped fresh mint

½ teaspoon ground nutmeg

salt and ground pepper to taste

½ lb (250 g) filo dough (20 sheets), thawed if frozen

½ cup (4 oz/125 g) unsalted butter, melted and cooled

MAKE-AHEAD TIP: These tiropites can be assembled up to 3 days in advance, covered, and refrigerated. Bake as directed just before serving.

Common all over Greece, stuffed filo pastries make a memorable meze. These small triangles are stuffed with feta and spinach. You might also see them stuffed with feta and herbs, or with lamb and spices and rolled into cigar shapes or tied like knots. Serve these pastries with a glass of ouzo over ice.

MAKES 30 TRIANGLES; SERVES 6

❀ Heat a large frying pan over medium-high heat. Add the spinach with only the rinsing water clinging to the leaves, cover, and cook until wilted, about 1 minute. Drain well on paper towels, then squeeze out as much of the remaining liquid as possible. Place in a large bowl and add the feta cheese; kefalotiri, Parmesan, or pecorino cheese; eggs; mint; and nutmeg. Stir well to combine. Season with salt and pepper.

❀ Preheat an oven to 375°F (190°C).

❀ Lightly butter a baking sheet. Cut the stack of filo sheets lengthwise into 3 equal strips. Remove 1 strip and cover the remaining filo with a slightly dampened kitchen towel to prevent it from drying out. Place the strip on a work surface and brush lightly with melted butter. Place another strip on top. Brush the second strip lightly with melted butter. Place a heaping teaspoonful of the filling about 1 inch (2.5 cm) in from the bottom of the strip. Fold the uncovered end over the filling on the diagonal to form a triangular shape. Bring the bottom of the triangle up against the straight edge. Continue folding in this manner until the tip of the strip is reached, forming a triangular pastry. Brush lightly with melted butter. Place on the prepared baking sheet. Repeat with the remaining filo and filling.

❀ Bake until golden, about 15 minutes. Remove from the oven and transfer to a platter. Serve immediately, warm, or at room temperature.

NUTRITIONAL ANALYSIS PER SERVING: Calories 454 (Kilojoules 1,907); Protein 17 g; Carbohydrates 25 g; Total Fat 32 g; Saturated Fat 19 g; Cholesterol 225 mg; Sodium 754 mg; Dietary Fiber 2 g

Country Salad

PREP TIME: 15 MINUTES

INGREDIENTS

4 small, ripe tomatoes, about 1¼ lb (625 g) total weight, cut into 1–1½-inch (2.5–4-cm) pieces

1 small red (Spanish) onion, cut into 1-inch (2.5-cm) dice

1 red bell pepper (capsicum), seeded and cut into 1–1½-inch (2.5–4-cm) pieces

1 English (hothouse) cucumber, cut into 1-inch (2.5-cm) pieces

5 tablespoons (2½ fl oz/75 ml) extra-virgin olive oil

3 tablespoons red wine vinegar

salt and ground pepper to taste

¾ lb (375 g) feta cheese

¾ cup (4 oz/125 g) Kalamata olives

1 teaspoon dried Greek oregano

In Greece, this familiar salad often includes crisp green tomatoes, which are surprisingly sweet, along with cucumbers, bell peppers, olives, and pungent feta. Cruets of fruity Greek olive oil and red wine vinegar are set out for diners to dress their own salads.

SERVES 6

❁ Toss the tomatoes, onion, bell pepper, and cucumber together. Drizzle with the olive oil and vinegar. Season with salt and pepper. Crumble the feta evenly over the top. Scatter the olives on top and sprinkle the salad with the oregano. Transfer to individual bowls and serve immediately.

NUTRITIONAL ANALYSIS PER SERVING: Calories 348 (Kilojoules 1,462); Protein 10 g; Carbohydrates 14 g; Total Fat 29 g; Saturated Fat 11 g; Cholesterol 51 mg; Sodium 984 mg; Dietary Fiber 3 g

Grape Leaves Stuffed with Rice and Currants

PREP TIME: 1¼ HOURS

COOKING TIME: 2 HOURS, PLUS 2 HOURS FOR COOLING

INGREDIENTS

1 jar (1 lb/500 g) grape leaves (about 6 dozen)

½ cup (4 fl oz/120 ml) extra-virgin olive oil

1 large yellow onion, minced

1 cup (7 oz/220 g) long-grain white rice

12 green (spring) onions, including tender green tops, thinly sliced

⅓ cup (2 oz/60 g) pine nuts

⅓ cup (2 oz/60 g) dried currants

¼ cup (⅓ oz/10 g) chopped fresh flat-leaf (Italian) parsley

3 tablespoons chopped fresh mint

3 tablespoons chopped fresh dill

¾ teaspoon salt, plus a pinch of salt

¼ teaspoon ground pepper

2 cups (16 fl oz/500 ml) water

½ cup (4 fl oz/125 ml) lemon juice

lemon slices

MAKES ABOUT 60 ROLLED GRAPE LEAVES

❀ Rinse the grape leaves in cold running water. Have ready a bowl filled with ice water. Bring a large saucepan three-fourths full of water to a boil. Add the grape leaves, a few at a time, and blanch for 1 minute. Using a slotted spoon, transfer to the ice water to cool. When all of the leaves have been blanched, drain and cut off the stems. Set aside.

❀ In a large frying pan over medium heat, warm ¼ cup (2 fl oz/60 ml) of the olive oil. Add the yellow onion and cook, stirring occasionally, until soft, about 7 minutes. Add the rice, green onions, and pine nuts and stir until the green onions soften, about 3 minutes. Add the currants, parsley, mint, dill, ¾ teaspoon salt, pepper, and 1 cup (8 fl oz/250 ml) of the water. Cover and cook over low heat until the water is absorbed and the rice is cooked, about 15 minutes.

❀ Line the bottom of a heavy 4-qt (4-l) saucepan with a few grape leaves. Sprinkle with the pinch of salt. To shape the rolled grape leaves, place a leaf, smooth side down, on a work surface. Put a heaping teaspoonful of the rice mixture near the base of the leaf at the stem end. Fold the stem end and sides over the filling and roll up toward the point of the leaf, forming a little bundle. Place, seam side down, in the prepared saucepan. Continue stuffing the grape leaves and adding them to the pan, packing them close together. When the bottom is completely covered, drizzle the layer with some of the remaining ¼ cup (2 fl oz/60 ml) olive oil and the lemon juice. Continue layering the stuffed grape leaves, drizzling each layer with olive oil and lemon juice, until all the filling is used. Add the remaining 1 cup (8 fl oz/250 ml) water and cover the top layer with a few leaves. Invert a small heatproof plate, smaller than the circumference of the pan, directly on top of the stuffed leaves.

❀ Cover the saucepan and bring to a boil over high heat. Reduce the heat to low, cover, and simmer until most of the liquid has been absorbed, about 1½ hours. Check the liquid in the bottom of the pan occasionally and add water as needed so the pan doesn't dry out. Remove from the heat and let the stuffed leaves stand in the pan to cool for about 2 hours.

❀ Transfer the stuffed grape leaves to a platter and garnish with lemon slices. Serve warm or at room temperature.

NUTRITIONAL ANALYSIS PER ROLLED GRAPE LEAF: Calories 45 (Kilojoules 189); Protein 1 g; Carbohydrates 4 g; Total Fat 2 g; Saturated Fat 0 g; Cholesterol 0 mg; Sodium 273 mg; Dietary Fiber 0 g

Fried Cod with Garlic Sauce

PREP TIME: 50 MINUTES

COOKING TIME: 10 MINUTES

INGREDIENTS

FOR THE SAUCE

6 oz (185 g) coarse country bread, crusts removed

4 cups (32 fl oz/1 l) water

½ cup (2 oz/60 g) walnuts

2 tablespoons white wine vinegar, or as needed

½ cup (4 fl oz/125 ml) olive oil

3 tablespoons mayonnaise

3 large cloves garlic, minced

salt and ground pepper to taste

2¼ cups (11½ oz/360 g) all-purpose (plain) flour

1 teaspoon baking powder

¼ teaspoon salt

¼ teaspoon ground pepper

1¼ cups (10 fl oz/310 ml) beer, at room temperature, or as needed

olive oil for deep-frying

2 lb (1 kg) rock cod or halibut fillets, cut into 1½-inch (4-cm) pieces

lemon wedges

PREP TIP: Once it's minced, garlic oxidizes and turns bitter if it sits for very long, so make this sauce within 6 hours of serving.

Skordalia, a popular full-flavored garlic sauce or dip, is traditionally thickened with bread if you are poor, potatoes if you have a bit of money, and nuts if you are wealthy. Enjoy it with roasted beets, Crisp Pita Chips (page 11), or this golden, crispy fish.

SERVES 6

❂ To make the sauce, place the bread in a bowl and pour the water over it. Immediately remove the bread from the water and squeeze it to remove the excess moisture. Discard the water.

❂ In a food processor or blender, process the walnuts almost to a paste. Add the soaked bread, 2 tablespoons vinegar, olive oil, mayonnaise, and garlic and purée to form a smooth paste. Season to taste with salt, pepper, and with more vinegar, if needed. Set aside.

❂ In a bowl, whisk together 1¼ cups (6½ oz/200 g) of the flour, the baking powder, salt, pepper, and 1¼ cups (10 fl oz/310 ml) beer. The batter should be the consistency of pourable pancake batter. Add more beer or some water, if necessary, to achieve the proper consistency.

❂ In a deep, heavy saucepan, pour in olive oil to a depth of 2 inches (5 cm) and heat to 375°F (190°C) on a deep-frying thermometer. Meanwhile, place the remaining 1 cup (5 oz/160 g) flour in a bowl. Dust the fish pieces with the flour, coating evenly and tapping off the excess, then dip the fish into the batter. Add the fish to the oil, in batches, and fry until golden and crispy, 1–2 minutes. Using a slotted spoon, transfer to paper towels to drain. Keep warm until all the fish is cooked.

❂ Transfer the fish to a warmed platter and garnish with lemon wedges. Serve the sauce alongside.

NUTRITIONAL ANALYSIS PER SERVING: Calories 718 (Kilojoules 3,016); Protein 36 g; Carbohydrates 54 g; Total Fat 38 g; Saturated Fat 5 g; Cholesterol 69 mg; Sodium 458 mg; Dietary Fiber 3 g

Mussels with Feta and Tomatoes

PREP TIME: 30 MINUTES

COOKING TIME: 35 MINUTES

INGREDIENTS

2 tablespoons olive oil

1 small yellow onion, minced

2 cups (12 oz/375 g) peeled, seeded, and chopped tomatoes (fresh or canned)

1 cup (8 fl oz/250 ml) dry white wine

¼ teaspoon dried oregano

pinch of red pepper flakes

1 teaspoon red wine vinegar

2 lb (1 kg) mussels, well scrubbed and debearded

6 oz (185 g) feta cheese, crumbled

salt and ground black pepper to taste

1 tablespoon coarsely chopped fresh flat-leaf (Italian) parsley

SERVING TIP: Serve with ouzo for the perfect accompaniment.

Feta is the most widely used cheese in Greece. The salty, white cheese is most commonly made from sheep's milk, and its name means "slice," after the way it is cut into blocks for sale. This meze can be made with other shellfish such as clams, shrimp (prawns), or scallops. Serve with plenty of crusty bread.

SERVES 6

❁ In a large frying pan over medium heat, warm the olive oil. Add the onion and cook, stirring occasionally, until soft, about 7 minutes. Raise the heat to high and add the tomatoes, wine, oregano, red pepper flakes, and vinegar. Stir well and bring to a boil. Reduce the heat to low and simmer uncovered, stirring occasionally, until thick, 20–30 minutes.

❁ Add the mussels, discarding any that fail to close to the touch, cover, and cook until most of the mussels open, 2–3 minutes. Uncover and, using tongs, transfer the opened mussels to a bowl. Re-cover and continue to cook until all the mussels have opened, a minute or so longer. Transfer the additional opened mussels to the bowl and discard any that failed to open. Remove the pan from the heat.

❁ When the mussels are just cool enough to handle, remove the meats from the shells and return them to the pan; discard the shells. Add the feta cheese to the pan as well and return the pan to medium heat. Bring to a gentle simmer and cook for 30 seconds, until the mussels are heated through and the cheese is softened. Season with salt and black pepper.

❁ Pour the mussels and their sauce onto a warmed platter and garnish with the parsley. Serve immediately.

NUTRITIONAL ANALYSIS PER SERVING: Calories 173 (Kilojoules 727); Protein 10 g; Carbohydrates 7 g; Total Fat 12 g; Saturated Fat 5 g; Cholesterol 38 mg; Sodium 450 mg; Dietary Fiber 1 g

Chicken Souvlaki

PREP TIME: 30 MINUTES, PLUS 1 HOUR FOR MARINATING

COOKING TIME: 1½ HOURS, PLUS PREPARING FIRE

INGREDIENTS

3 tablespoons extra-virgin olive oil

2 tablespoons dry white wine

1 tablespoon lemon juice

¼ cup (1½ oz/45 g) minced yellow onion

1 clove garlic, minced

2 bay leaves, broken or chopped into tiny pieces

1 teaspoon dried oregano

salt and ground pepper to taste

1 lb (500 g) skinless, boneless chicken, cut into 1-inch (2.5-cm) pieces

lemon wedges

flat-leaf (Italian) parsley leaves

COOKING TIP: These skewers can also be made with 1 pound (500 g) firm-fleshed fish fillets such as tuna or swordfish, cut into 1-inch (2.5-cm) chunks.

Visitors to Greece will find chicken, pork, lamb, and beef souvlaki served at streetside stands and restaurant tables alike. They are terrific straight from the skewer with just a squeeze of lemon, or stuffed into pita bread with Yogurt Dip with Garlic, Mint, and Dill (page 85). Serve with the same dry white wine used in the marinade. A broiler (griller) can be used, but the smoky charcoal flavor will be lost.

SERVES 6

❂ In a bowl, stir together the olive oil, wine, lemon juice, onion, garlic, bay leaves, oregano, salt, and pepper. Add the chicken pieces and turn to coat evenly. Cover and refrigerate for at least 1 hour or for up to overnight.

❂ Prepare a medium-hot fire in a charcoal grill. At the same time, put 6 bamboo skewers in water to cover.

❂ Remove the chicken pieces from the marinade and drain the skewers. Thread the chicken pieces onto the skewers, dividing the pieces evenly among them. Place on the grill rack 4–5 inches (10–13 cm) from the fire and grill, turning once, until the chicken is opaque throughout, 3–4 minutes on each side. Season with salt and pepper.

❂ Transfer to a warmed platter and garnish with lemon wedges and parsley. Serve immediately.

NUTRITIONAL ANALYSIS PER SERVING: Calories 123 (Kilojoules 517); Protein 16 g; Carbohydrates 1 g; Total Fat 6 g; Saturated Fat 1 g; Cholesterol 53 mg; Sodium 59 mg; Dietary Fiber 0 g

Yogurt Dip with Garlic, Mint, and Dill

PREP TIME: 40 MINUTES, PLUS 4 HOURS FOR DRAINING

INGREDIENTS

2 cups (1 lb/500 g) plain yogurt

about ½ English (hothouse) cucumber, peeled, halved, and seeded

salt

4 cloves garlic, mashed in a mortar or minced

1 tablespoon chopped fresh mint

1 tablespoon chopped fresh dill

1 tablespoon extra-virgin olive oil

2–3 teaspoons lemon juice

MAKE-AHEAD TIP: You can make the dip up to 1 day in advance, but do not add the garlic. Cover and refrigerate, then add the garlic the day of serving.

This tangy dip is called *tzatziki* in Greece, home to some of the best yogurt in the world. Here, it is used in a heady mixture that can be served as a dip with wedges of pita bread or tucked into a pita round with Chicken Souvlaki (page 83).

MAKES ABOUT 2 CUPS (1 LB/500 G); SERVES 6

❂ Line a sieve with cheesecloth (muslin) and place over a bowl. Spoon the yogurt into the sieve and refrigerate for 4 hours to drain.

❂ Meanwhile, using the large holes on a handheld grater-shredder, grate enough cucumber to measure 1 cup (4 oz/125 g). Spread out the grated cucumber on paper towels, salt lightly, and let drain for 15 minutes.

❂ In a bowl, combine the yogurt, cucumber, garlic, mint, dill, olive oil, and lemon juice to taste. Stir to mix well, then season with salt.

❂ Transfer to a bowl and serve.

NUTRITIONAL ANALYSIS PER SERVING: Calories 79 (Kilojoules 332); Protein 4 g; Carbohydrates 2 g; Total Fat 6 g; Saturated Fat 3 g; Cholesterol 16 mg; Sodium 42 mg; Dietary Fiber 0 g

Saganaki

PREP TIME: 10 MINUTES

COOKING TIME: 10 MINUTES

INGREDIENTS

olive oil for frying

½-lb (250-g) piece kefalotiri cheese, cut into sticks about ½ inch (12 mm) thick

1 cup (5 oz/155 g) all-purpose (plain) flour

¼ cup (2 fl oz/60 ml) lemon juice

6 lemon wedges

12 Kalamata olives

SERVING TIP: For the best texture, serve these the moment they come out of the frying pan.

This fried cheese appetizer takes its name from the pan in which it is traditionally cooked. Kefalotiri, a sheep's milk cheese with a dense texture and a marked tang, is commonly used in this dish. If it is unavailable, Italian fontinella, Gruyère, or pecorino romano cheese can be substituted.

SERVES 6

❀ In a small frying pan, pour in olive oil to a depth of ¼ inch (6 mm) and place over medium-high heat. As soon as the surface of the oil ripples, reduce the heat to medium-low.

❀ Meanwhile, fill a bowl three-fourths full of water and slip the cheese sticks into it. Place the flour in another bowl. Remove the cheese from the water and immediately place it in the flour, dusting both sides evenly. Do not tap off the excess flour.

❀ Working in batches, slip the cheese into the hot oil in a single layer and fry, turning once with a fork, until golden and crispy, 1–2 minutes on each side. The sticks should be soft all the way through, but not melting. Using the fork, transfer to a warmed platter and, working quickly, repeat with the remaining cheese sticks.

❀ Drizzle with the lemon juice and garnish with the lemon wedges and olives. Serve piping hot.

NUTRITIONAL ANALYSIS PER SERVING: Calories 337 (Kilojoules 1,415); Protein 14 g; Carbohydrates 22 g; Total Fat 22 g; Saturated Fat 8 g; Cholesterol 42 mg; Sodium 310 mg; Dietary Fiber 1 g

Artichokes Stewed with Lemon and Garlic

PREP TIME: 45 MINUTES

COOKING TIME: 10 MINUTES, PLUS 1 HOUR FOR COOLING

INGREDIENTS

4 lemons

36 small artichokes, 1–2 oz (30–60 g) each

20 cloves garlic, halved

10 fresh thyme sprigs

5 bay leaves

1½ teaspoons coarse salt

¾ cup (6 fl oz/180 ml) olive oil

1 teaspoon chopped fresh flat-leaf (Italian) parsley

STORAGE TIP: Divide the artichokes between two 1-qt (1-l) sterilized jars. Add enough of the remaining liquid to immerse the artichokes completely. Cover tightly and store in the refrigerator for up to 2 weeks.

Artichokes are thorny blossoms that, if not picked, turn into lovely purple flowers. Harvested in the early spring and then again, in smaller amounts, in the fall, artichokes are a common sight on any meze table. In this recipe, they are dressed with familiar Greek ingredients—lemon, bay, garlic, and olive oil.

MAKES 2 QT (2 L); SERVES 12

⊛ Using a vegetable peeler, remove the zest from the lemons and set aside.

⊛ Fill a large bowl three-fourths full with water. Halve 1 lemon and squeeze the juice into the water. Working with 1 artichoke at a time, break off the tough outer leaves to reach the pale green, tender inner leaves. Trim away the tough, dark green layer around the base. Cut off the top one-half of the artichoke, including all of the prickly leaf points. Trim off the end of the stem, then pare the stem to reveal the light green center. Cut the artichoke in half lengthwise and slip the halves into the lemon water. Trim the remaining artichokes in the same way.

⊛ Drain the artichokes and place them in a saucepan. Halve the remaining 3 lemons and squeeze the juice into the saucepan. Add the reserved lemon zest, the garlic, thyme sprigs, bay leaves, salt, and olive oil. Add water just to cover and place a piece of parchment (baking) paper the diameter of the pan on top of the artichokes. Weight the parchment with a heatproof plate that rests directly on the artichokes. Bring to a boil over medium-high heat, reduce the heat to medium, and simmer for 5 minutes. Remove from the heat and let cool completely in the pan, about 1 hour or until tender when pierced with a knife.

⊛ Using a slotted spoon, transfer the artichokes to a bowl. Garnish with the parsley and serve at room temperature.

NUTRITIONAL ANALYSIS PER SERVING: Calories 122 (Kilojoules 512); Protein 2 g; Carbohydrates 8 g; Total Fat 10 g; Saturated Fat 1 g; Cholesterol 0 mg; Sodium 187 mg; Dietary Fiber 3 g

Grilled Lamb Kabobs with Mint-Yogurt Sauce

PREP TIME: 35 MINUTES, PLUS 2 HOURS FOR DRAINING

COOKING TIME: 10 MINUTES, PLUS PREPARING FIRE

INGREDIENTS

¾ cup (6 oz/185 g) plain yogurt

1 lb (500 g) lamb cut from the leg, shoulder, or loin, trimmed of fat and cut into 1-inch (2.5-cm) pieces

3 tablespoons extra-virgin olive oil

salt and ground pepper to taste

3 tablespoons chopped fresh mint, plus sprigs for garnish

1 clove garlic, minced

3 tablespoons lemon juice

6 lemon wedges

COOKING TIP: Add 1 red bell pepper (capsicum), roasted, peeled, and puréed, to the sauce.

Kabobs are made all over the Mediterranean, and in the eastern Mediterranean, lamb is the meat of choice. If you like, remove the hot lamb from the skewers, tuck into pita wedges, and drizzle with the sauce. Roasted vegetables, such as bell peppers (capsicums), eggplants (aubergines), and zucchini (courgettes) are often slipped into the pita as well.

SERVES 6

❁ Line a fine-mesh sieve with cheesecloth (muslin) and place over a bowl. Spoon the yogurt into the sieve. Cover and refrigerate for 2 hours to drain.

❁ Prepare a medium-hot fire in a charcoal grill. At the same time, put 6 bamboo skewers in water to cover.

❁ In a bowl, combine the lamb and 2 tablespoons of the olive oil. Season with salt and pepper. Toss to coat evenly.

❁ In a small bowl, combine the drained yogurt, the remaining 1 tablespoon olive oil, the chopped mint, the garlic, and the lemon juice. Stir to mix well. Season with salt and pepper. Set aside.

❁ Drain the skewers and thread the lamb pieces onto them, dividing them evenly. Place on the grill rack 4–5 inches (10–13 cm) from the fire and grill until browned on the first side, about 5 minutes. Turn the kabobs and continue to grill until browned on the second side and medium-rare at the center, 4–5 minutes longer, or until done to your liking.

❁ Transfer the kabobs to a serving platter, season with salt and pepper, and drizzle the yogurt sauce over them. Garnish with the lemon wedges and mint sprigs. Serve immediately, warm, or at room temperature.

NUTRITIONAL ANALYSIS PER SERVING: Calories 184 (Kilojoules 773); Protein 17 g; Carbohydrates 3 g; Total Fat 12 g; Saturated Fat 3 g; Cholesterol 54 mg; Sodium 56 mg; Dietary Fiber 0 g

Hummus

PREP TIME: 30 MINUTES, PLUS 4 HOURS FOR SOAKING

COOKING TIME: 1 HOUR

INGREDIENTS

1⅓ cups (9 oz/280 g) dried chickpeas (garbanzo beans)

½ cup (4 fl oz/125 ml) lemon juice, or as needed

½ cup (5 oz/155 g) tahini *(see note)*

4 tablespoons (2 fl oz/60 ml) extra-virgin olive oil

5 cloves garlic, minced

¾ teaspoon salt, or as needed

¼ teaspoon ground cumin

2 teaspoons chopped fresh flat-leaf (Italian) parsley

large pinch of paprika

6 lemon wedges or radishes

¼ cup (1¼ oz/37 g) brine-cured black olives such as Kalamata

SERVING TIP: Serve several salads or dips at the same time with pita bread: Hummus, Baba Ghanoush (page 100), Turkish Tomato and Chile Relish (page 96), and Feta Salad with Cucumbers, Green and Red Onions, and Mint (page 103).

Tahini, a stiff paste made from toasted ground sesame seeds, is one of the most important ingredients in Middle Eastern cooking. Here it is used to make a garlicky chickpea purée flavored with cumin. If you would like a spicier mix, add a little cayenne pepper. Serve with warm pita or crusty bread.

SERVES 6

⊛ Pick over and discard any misshapen peas or stones. Rinse the chickpeas and drain. Place in a bowl, add water to cover generously, and let soak for at least 4 hours or for up to overnight.

⊛ Drain the chickpeas and place in a saucepan with water to cover by 2 inches (5 cm). Bring to a boil over high heat, reduce the heat to low, and simmer, uncovered, until the skins crack and the chickpeas are very tender, about 1 hour. Remove from the heat and drain, reserving the liquid.

⊛ In a food processor or blender, combine the chickpeas, ½ cup (4 fl oz/125 ml) lemon juice, the tahini, 3 tablespoons of the olive oil, the garlic, ¾ teaspoon salt, and the cumin. Process until a soft, creamy paste forms. Taste and adjust with salt and lemon juice, if needed.

⊛ Transfer the purée to a serving bowl and spread with the back of a spoon to form a shallow well. Drizzle with the remaining 1 tablespoon olive oil. Sprinkle with the parsley and paprika. Garnish with the lemon wedges or radishes and the olives and serve.

NUTRITIONAL ANALYSIS PER SERVING: Calories 404 (Kilojoules 1,697); Protein 13 g; Carbohydrates 35 g; Total Fat 26 g; Saturated Fat 4 g; Cholesterol 0 mg; Sodium 440 mg; Dietary Fiber 5 g

Tabbouleh

PREP TIME: 30 MINUTES, PLUS 24 HOURS FOR REFRIGERATING

INGREDIENTS

¾ cup (4½ oz/140 g) medium-fine bulgur

1 cup (8 fl oz/250 ml) lemon juice, or as needed

½ cup (4 fl oz/125 ml) extra-virgin olive oil

5 cloves garlic, minced

8 green (spring) onions, including tender green tops, diced

1 cup (1½ oz/45 g) chopped fresh flat-leaf (Italian) parsley

⅓ cup (½ oz/15 g) chopped fresh mint

4 large, ripe tomatoes, diced

1 English (hothouse) cucumber, peeled, halved, seeded, and diced

2½ teaspoons salt

¼ teaspoon ground pepper

1 head romaine (cos) lettuce, leaves separated, or 3 pita bread rounds, heated and cut into wedges

Bulgur and tomatoes are the main components of this popular Middle Eastern summer salad. Eat it as the Lebanese do, scooping it up with romaine leaves instead of a fork. Alternatively, capture mouthfuls with wedges of pita bread. Tabbouleh is best when made at least 1 day in advance of serving so that the flavors have time to develop.

SERVES 6

❋ Place the bulgur on the bottom of a large salad bowl. In a small bowl, whisk together the 1 cup (8 fl oz/250 ml) lemon juice, olive oil, and garlic and drizzle over the bulgur. In the following order, layer the green onions, parsley, mint, tomatoes, and cucumber on top of the bulgur. Season the top layer with 1½ teaspoons of the salt and the ¼ teaspoon pepper and cover with plastic wrap. Refrigerate for at least 24 hours or for up to 48 hours.

❋ Bring to room temperature and toss together. Taste and season with the remaining 1 teaspoon salt and more lemon juice, if needed. Serve with the romaine leaves or warmed pita bread.

NUTRITIONAL ANALYSIS PER SERVING: Calories 393 (Kilojoules 1,651); Protein 9 g; Carbohydrates 50 g; Total Fat 20 g; Saturated Fat 3 g; Cholesterol 0 mg; Sodium 1,175 mg; Dietary Fiber 9 g

Turkish Tomato and Chile Relish

PREP TIME: 35 MINUTES, PLUS 1 HOUR FOR DRAINING

INGREDIENTS

3 tomatoes, about 1¼ lb (625 g) total weight, finely chopped

5 tablespoons (2½ oz/75 g) tomato paste

2 tablespoons extra-virgin olive oil

4 green Anaheim chiles, seeded and minced

½ cup (3 oz/90 g) minced yellow onion

3 tablespoons chopped fresh flat-leaf (Italian) parsley

½–1 teaspoon red pepper flakes

salt and ground black pepper to taste

In summer, when tomatoes are sweet from the vine, Turkish cooks prepare this simple relish. Sometimes it is served as a salad. It is also very good with Crisp Pita Chips (page 11) or bread, accompanied by a glass of wine or raki. If you have any left over, offer it as a condiment with grilled chicken breasts.

SERVES 6

❁ Place the tomatoes in a fine-mesh sieve set over a bowl. Let drain for 1 hour. Discard the juice or reserve for another use.

❁ In a bowl, combine the tomatoes, tomato paste, olive oil, Anaheim chiles, onion, parsley, and the red pepper flakes to taste in a bowl. Stir to mix well. Season with salt and black pepper.

❁ Transfer to a serving bowl and serve at room temperature.

NUTRITIONAL ANALYSIS PER SERVING: Calories 84 (Kilojoules 353); Protein 2 g; Carbohydrates 10 g; Total Fat 5 g; Saturated Fat 1 g; Cholesterol 0 mg; Sodium 104 mg; Dietary Fiber 2 g

MAKE-AHEAD TIP: The relish can be made 1 day in advance, covered, and refrigerated. Bring to room temperature before serving.

Green Beans Stewed with Tomatoes and Garlic

PREP TIME: 25 MINUTES

COOKING TIME: 50 MINUTES

INGREDIENTS

2 tablespoons olive oil

1 small yellow onion, chopped

4 cloves garlic, thinly sliced

1 lb (500 g) green beans, trimmed

2 cups (12 oz/375 g) peeled, seeded, and chopped tomatoes (fresh or canned)

2 tablespoons chopped fresh flat-leaf (Italian) parsley

salt and ground pepper to taste

Green beans that are just past their prime work well for this dish. Pair them with Grilled Lamb Kabobs with Mint-Yogurt Sauce (page 90).

SERVES 6

❂ In a large frying pan over medium heat, warm the olive oil. Add the onion and cook, stirring occasionally, until soft, about 7 minutes. Add the garlic and stir for 1 minute to release its fragrance. Raise the heat to high and add the beans, tomatoes, and parsley. Bring to a simmer, reduce the heat to low, cover, and cook until the beans are very tender and soft, about 30 minutes. Uncover, raise the heat to medium, and continue to cook until most of the liquid has evaporated, about 10 minutes longer. Season with salt and pepper.

❂ Transfer to a serving plate and serve hot or at room temperature.

NUTRITIONAL ANALYSIS PER SERVING: Calories 83 (Kilojoules 349); Protein 2 g; Carbohydrates 10 g; Total Fat 5 g; Saturated Fat 1 g; Cholesterol 0 mg; Sodium 10 mg; Dietary Fiber 2 g

Baba Ghanoush

PREP TIME: 25 MINUTES

COOKING TIME: 35 MINUTES, PLUS PREPARING FIRE

INGREDIENTS

1 large eggplant (aubergine)

¼ cup (2½ oz/75 g) tahini, or to taste

3 cloves garlic, minced

¼ cup (2 fl oz/60 ml) lemon juice, or to taste

large pinch of ground cumin

salt to taste

1 tablespoon extra-virgin olive oil

1 tablespoon chopped fresh flat-leaf (Italian) parsley

¼ cup (1¼ oz/37 g) brine-cured black olives such as Kalamata

COOKING TIP: If you like, you can cook the eggplant completely in the oven instead of first blackening it on the grill. Put the eggplant in a preheated 350°F (180°C) oven and cook until soft, 30–40 minutes. It won't have the same smoky flavor, but it will still be delicious. You can also lay the eggplant directly on the gas jet of your stove and blacken and blister as described for the charcoal grill.

This creamy mixture is made with smoky, fire-roasted eggplant, tahini (sesame-seed paste), lemon juice, and plenty of minced garlic. Serve with warmed pita wedges or crackers.

SERVES 6

❁ Prepare a medium-hot fire in a charcoal grill. Preheat an oven to 375°F (190°C).

❁ Prick the eggplant with a fork in several places and place on the grill rack 4–5 inches (10–13 cm) from the fire. Grill, turning frequently, until the skin blackens and blisters and the flesh just begins to feel soft, 10–15 minutes. Transfer the eggplant to a baking sheet and bake until very soft, 15–20 minutes. Remove from the oven, let cool slightly, and peel off and discard the skin. Place the eggplant flesh in a bowl.

❁ Using a fork, mash the eggplant to a paste. Add ¼ cup (2½ oz/75 g) tahini, garlic, ¼ cup (2 fl oz/60 ml) lemon juice, and cumin and mix well. Season with salt, then taste and adjust with more lemon juice and/or tahini.

❁ Transfer the mixture to a serving bowl and spread it with the back of a spoon to form a shallow well. Drizzle the olive oil over the top and sprinkle with the parsley. Place the olives around the sides. Serve at room temperature.

NUTRITIONAL ANALYSIS PER SERVING: Calories 142 (Kilojoules 596); Protein 3 g; Carbohydrates 12 g; Total Fat 10 g; Saturated Fat 1 g; Cholesterol 0 mg; Sodium 127 mg; Dietary Fiber 3 g

Feta Salad with Cucumbers, Green and Red Onions, and Mint

PREP TIME: 25 MINUTES

INGREDIENTS

½ lb (250 g) feta cheese

2–3 tablespoons lemon juice

1 tablespoon extra-virgin olive oil

salt and ground pepper to taste

1 English (hothouse) cucumber, peeled, halved, seeded, and thickly sliced

¼ cup (2 oz/60 g) diced red (Spanish) onion (¼-inch/6-mm dice)

6 green (spring) onions, white portion plus 2 inches (5 cm) of tender green tops, thinly sliced

3 tablespoons chopped fresh mint, plus sprigs for garnish

2 tablespoons chopped fresh parsley

2 tablespoons chopped fresh dill, plus sprigs for garnish

3 pita bread rounds, heated and cut into wedges

SERVING TIP: This versatile dish can be served on a meze table or as a salad alongside a main course of grilled butterflied leg of lamb.

This recipe could not be easier: just crumble and chop. Toss it all together, stir for a second, and it is ready. Use the warm pita bread for scooping it up.

SERVES 6

❀ Crumble the feta into a bowl. Add the lemon juice to taste, olive oil, salt, and pepper and toss together with a fork. Add the cucumber, red onion, green onions, and the chopped mint, parsley, and dill. Toss together to mix well.

❀ Transfer to a serving plate and garnish with dill and mint sprigs. Serve with the pita wedges.

NUTRITIONAL ANALYSIS PER SERVING: Calories 222 (Kilojoules 932); Protein 9 g; Carbohydrates 23 g; Total Fat 11 g; Saturated Fat 6 g; Cholesterol 34 mg; Sodium 593 mg; Dietary Fiber 1 g

Fattoush

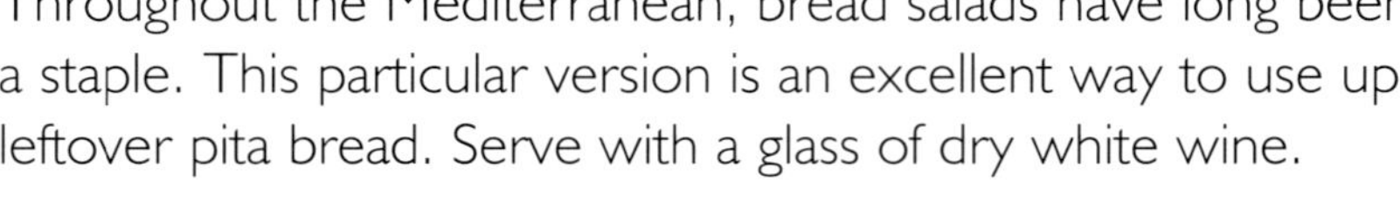

Throughout the Mediterranean, bread salads have long been a staple. This particular version is an excellent way to use up leftover pita bread. Serve with a glass of dry white wine.

PREP TIME: 30 MINUTES

COOKING TIME: 15 MINUTES

INGREDIENTS

2 pita bread rounds, 3–4 days old and each 8 inches (20 cm) in diameter

1 English (hothouse) cucumber, peeled, halved, seeded, and diced

salt for sprinkling cucumbers, plus salt to taste

3 tomatoes, about 1¼ lb (625 g) total weight, seeded and diced

6 green (spring) onions, including tender green tops, cut into slices ¼ inch (6 mm) thick

1 green bell pepper (capsicum), seeded and diced

⅓ cup (½ oz/15 g) coarsely chopped fresh mint

¼ cup (⅓ oz/10 g) coarsely chopped fresh flat-leaf (Italian) parsley

¼ cup (⅓ oz/10 g) coarsely chopped fresh cilantro (fresh coriander)

ground pepper to taste

2 large cloves garlic, minced

¼ cup (2 fl oz/60 ml) lemon juice

⅓ cup (3 fl oz/80 ml) extra-virgin olive oil

SERVES 6

- Preheat an oven to 375°F (190°C).
- Split each pita bread into 2 rounds by separating it along the outside seam, then tear the rounds into 1-inch (2.5-cm) pieces. Spread the pieces out on a baking sheet. Bake until lightly golden and dry, 10–15 minutes. Remove from the oven and place in a bowl.
- Meanwhile, spread the diced cucumber on paper towels in a single layer, salt lightly, and let drain for 15 minutes. Transfer to a colander, place under cold running water for a few seconds, and then pat dry with clean paper towels.
- Add the cucumber, tomatoes, green onions, bell pepper, mint, parsley, and cilantro to the bread. Season with salt and pepper and toss well.
- In a small bowl, whisk together the garlic, lemon juice, and olive oil. Season with salt and pepper. Drizzle over the vegetables and bread and toss well.
- Transfer the salad to a platter and serve at once.

NUTRITIONAL ANALYSIS PER SERVING: Calories 225 (Kilojoules 945); Protein 4 g; Carbohydrates 25 g; Total Fat 13 g; Saturated Fat 2 g; Cholesterol 0 mg; Sodium 170 mg; Dietary Fiber 3 g

SERVING TIP: Sumac, a spice made from a type of Middle Eastern berry, imparts a slightly fruity, astringent flavor to foods and is often sprinkled onto this salad before serving. Look for it in Middle Eastern stores.

Turkish Flat Bread with Lamb and Tomatoes

PREP TIME: 45 MINUTES, PLUS 1 HOUR FOR RISING

COOKING TIME: 50 MINUTES

INGREDIENTS

FOR THE DOUGH

½ teaspoon active dry yeast

¾ cup (6 fl oz/180 ml) warm water (115°F/46°C)

2 tablespoons olive oil

1 tablespoon unsalted butter, melted and cooled

2¼ cups (11½ oz/360 g) bread (hard-wheat) flour

½ teaspoon salt

FOR THE TOPPING

3 tablespoons pine nuts

1½ tablespoons olive oil

1 small yellow onion, minced

¾ lb (375 g) ground (minced) lamb

¾ cup (4½ oz/140 g) peeled, seeded, chopped, and drained tomatoes

2 tablespoons tomato paste

¼ cup (⅓ oz/10 g) chopped fresh flat-leaf (Italian) parsley

¼ teaspoon each ground cinnamon and ground allspice

⅛ teaspoon ground cloves

½ teaspoon each salt and ground black pepper

¼ teaspoon red pepper flakes

1 tablespoon lemon juice

2 tablespoons unsalted butter, melted and cooled

These round, thin Turkish "pizzas," or *lamachun,* are traditionally rolled up into cylinders for easy eating as a favorite street food. You can also cut them into wedges for serving on the meze table.

MAKES 12 SMALL FLAT BREADS; SERVES 6

❁ To make the dough, in a bowl, stir together the yeast and ¼ cup (2 fl oz/60 ml) of the warm water. Let stand until foamy, about 10 minutes. Add the remaining ½ cup (4 fl oz/120 ml) warm water, the olive oil, butter, flour, and salt. Stir until the dough gathers together in a ball and pulls away from the sides of the bowl. Turn out onto a floured work surface and knead until smooth and elastic, 7–10 minutes. Place the dough in an oiled bowl, turning to coat with oil. Cover the bowl with plastic wrap, transfer to a warm place (about 75°F/24°C), and let the dough rise until doubled in bulk, about 1 hour.

❁ Meanwhile, make the topping: In a small, dry frying pan over medium heat, toast the pine nuts, stirring constantly, until golden and fragrant, about 1 minute. Remove from the heat and transfer to a plate. In a large frying pan over medium-high heat, warm the olive oil. Add the onion and cook, stirring occasionally, until soft, about 7 minutes. Add the lamb, tomatoes, tomato paste, parsley, pine nuts, cinnamon, allspice, cloves, salt, black pepper, and red pepper flakes and cook slowly uncovered, breaking up the lamb with a wooden spoon, until the mixture is almost dry, about 8 minutes. Stir in the lemon juice and let cool.

❁ Preheat an oven to 500°F (260°C). Oil 2 baking sheets. Turn out the dough onto a floured work surface and divide into 12 equal pieces. Roll out 6 pieces into rounds 7–8 inches (18–20 cm) in diameter and 1/16 inch (2 mm) thick. Place 3 rounds on each prepared baking sheet and let rest for 10 minutes. Divide half of the filling evenly among the rounds, spreading it to the edges. It will not completely cover the dough. Drizzle evenly with half of the butter.

❁ Bake until lightly golden around the edges but still soft enough to roll up, 5–7 minutes. (If your oven is too small to hold both baking sheets on the middle rack, bake in batches.) Remove from the oven and roll up each round into a cylinder. Serve immediately. Repeat with the remaining dough pieces and topping.

NUTRITIONAL ANALYSIS PER SERVING: Calories 535 (Kilojoules 2,247); Protein 18 g; Carbohydrates 46 g; Total Fat 31 g; Saturated Fat 11 g; Cholesterol 57 mg; Sodium 469 mg; Dietary Fiber 2 g

GLOSSARY

ANCHOVY FILLETS

A small, slender relative of the sardine, the anchovy is most commonly preserved by salting its fillets and then packing them in olive oil. Whole anchovies, packed in salt alone, must be filleted and rinsed before using.

BEANS, DRIED

Eaten hot or cold, whole or puréed, cooked dried beans are a popular ingredient in Mediterranean small plates. Among the many varieties available, two of the most popular are Italian **cannellini,** small, white, thin-skinned, oval beans, for which **Great Northern** or **white (navy) beans** may be substituted, and **chickpeas (garbanzo beans),** buff-colored members of the pea family about the size and shape of small hazelnuts (filberts). **Chickpea flour,** found in some Italian, Middle Eastern, Indian, and Pakistani markets, is used for thickening and in coatings for deep-fried foods.

BELL PEPPERS

As they ripen, these mild bell-shaped peppers, also known as capsicums, change from green to red or to other colors such as orange or yellow, and their flavors, somewhat sharp when green, sweeten and mellow.

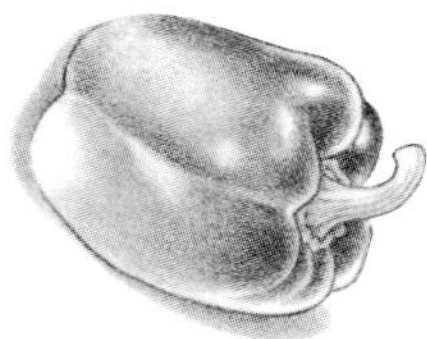

BREAD

Good-quality fresh-baked bread is now widely available at specialty bakeries and well-stocked food stores. **Coarse country loaves,** also sometimes referred to as peasant or rustic loaves, are white loaves made from unbleached wheat flour, with a good chewy or crisp crust and a robust, firm-textured crumb. **French bread,** while sometimes of the coarse country type, is more often a good-quality loaf made from bleached white flour, with a finer, lighter crumb and softer crust. **Pita,** a Middle Eastern bread sometimes called pocket bread, is baked in individual flat ovals or rounds whose two horizontal layers separate, making them ideal for stuffing or for serving with appetizer dips or spreads.

BREAD CRUMBS, FINE DRIED

To make fine dried bread crumbs, trim away the crusts from fresh French- or Italian-style white bread (but not sourdough). Put the bread in a food processor and process to make soft fresh crumbs. Spread them on a baking sheet and bake in a preheated 325°F (165°C) oven until dry, about 15 minutes. Let the crumbs cool, then process again until fine. Return to the oven and bake, stirring once or twice, until lightly colored, about 15 minutes.

BULGUR

Also known as burghul, this popular Middle Eastern ingredient consists of wheat berries that have been steamed, dried, partially stripped of their bran, and then cracked into particles ranging from fine to coarse. Used in salads, pilafs, stuffings, and ground (minced) meat mixtures, bulgur has a robust nutlike flavor and chewy texture.

CAPERS

The buds of a bush common to the Mediterranean, capers are picked when fully developed but still unopened, then preserved either by salting or by pickling in a vinegar-and-salt

EQUIPMENT

MORTAR AND PESTLE
Used in combination, this heavy bowl (the mortar) and handheld cylindrical pounder (the pestle) form an ideal tool for pounding whole fresh or dried seasonings into powders or pastes. Mortars and pestles are made in many styles.

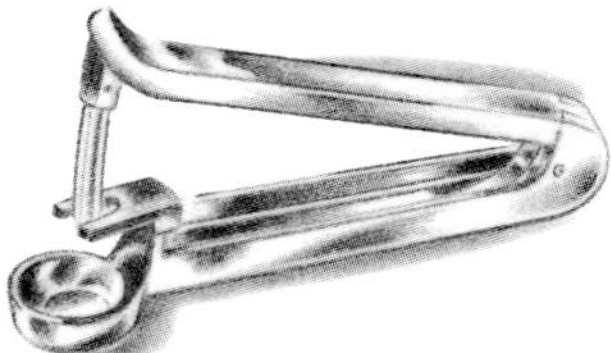

OLIVE PITTER
This specialized kitchen tool, sometimes also labeled a cherry pitter, grips an olive in its cup-shaped holder and, with a squeeze of its handle, pushes out the pit.

PIZZA STONE
This porous stone slab, made of the same clay used to line commercial pottery kilns, absorbs moisture in a home oven to produce a dry heat resembling that found in a brick bakery oven. The result is crisp crusts for pizzas and other bread doughs.

brine. Used whole or chopped, they make a sharp-tasting savory flavoring or garnish.

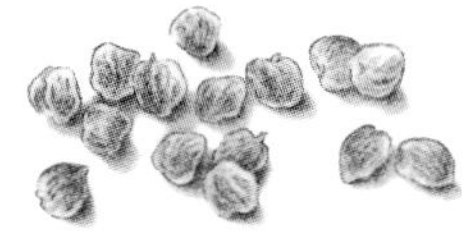

CUCUMBERS, ENGLISH (HOTHOUSE)
This variety of cucumber is noted for its long, narrow shape and mild flavor. More

importantly, it has a smooth, thin skin that is less bitter than those of other varieties, and therefore does not require peeling. It is nearly seedless.

CURRANTS, DRIED
Resembling tiny raisins, these dried fruits produced from a variety of small grape, the Zante, have a stronger, tarter flavor than raisins. They are found in the baking section of well-stocked food stores.

FAVA BEANS, FRESH
A specialty of springtime, these fresh shelling beans, also known as broad beans, resemble large lima beans and are especially prized for their sweet flavor when young and tender. Easily shelled by splitting the pod along its seam, the beans also usually require peeling of their outer skins, which, although edible, are sometimes tough.

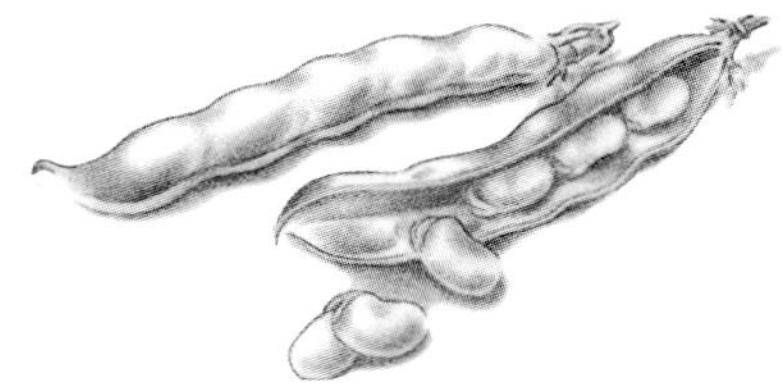

FILO DOUGH
This Middle Eastern flour-and-water pastry consists of fragile, tissue-thin leaves that are usually layered and used as wrappers for sweet or savory fillings. Sold in the freezer section of well-stocked food stores, or fresh in many Middle Eastern markets, the dough must be handled carefully to avoid tearing.

GARLIC
For the best flavor, buy no more of this pungent seasoning, a member of the onion family, than you will use in 1–2 weeks, storing the garlic in a cool, dry place. Separate individual cloves as needed, loosening their peels by crushing them gently with the side of a large knife or other heavy object.

GRAPE LEAVES
The leaves of grapevines are commonly used in Greece and the Middle East as edible wrappers for savory fillings of rice, meat, vegetables, and other ingredients. Specialty-food shops and well-stocked food stores sell them bottled in brine, requiring only rinsing and removal of tough stems before use. If using fresh leaves, make sure they are pesticide free, and blanch or steam briefly to soften before use.

CHEESES
Many cheeses from Mediterranean countries are popular ingredients in the region's small plates. Those called for in this book include:

FETA
Tangy, crumbly white cheese from Greece, traditionally made from sheep's milk.

FONTINA
Popular Italian cow's milk cheese with a firm, creamy texture and delicate, slightly nutty taste. The best version is produced in Val d'Aosta, a valley high in the Italian Alps near Switzerland.

GORGONZOLA
Italian variety of blue-veined cheese prized for its pungent flavor and creamy texture. Young Gorgonzola is particularly mild and is referred to as Dolcelatte, or "sweet milk."

KEFALOTIRI
Popular Greek sheep's milk cheese, most commonly aged until hard and yellow and used for cooking.

MANCHEGO
Rich-tasting Spanish sheep's milk cheese, usually sold cured *(curado)* for 3 to 13 weeks or aged *(viejo)* for more than 3 months.

MOZZARELLA, FRESH
A rindless Italian white cheese with a mild taste and soft but dense texture, mozzarella made in the traditional way from water buffalo's milk may be found fresh, floating in water, in well-stocked food stores and Italian delicatessens. If only cow's milk mozzarella is available, look for balls sold in water, often labeled *fior di latte,* rather than dry-packed in plastic.

PARMESAN
Italian cow's milk cheese aged to a sharp, salty flavor and firm texture. Look for Parmigiano-Reggiano®, the finest variety.

PECORINO
May apply to any Italian sheep's milk cheese, but most often refers to aged pecorino romano, traditionally produced near Rome and used for grating.

HERBS

Many different herbs, both fresh and dried, may be used to add flavor, aroma, and color to a wide variety of small plates. Those called for in this book include:

BASIL

Best enjoyed when fresh, this tender-leaved herb has a spicy-sweet flavor that especially complements dishes featuring tomatoes.

BAY LEAVES

The whole leaves of the bay laurel tree have a pungent, spicy flavor. Seek out the French variety, which has a milder, sweeter flavor than bay leaves from California.

CILANTRO

Also known as fresh coriander and Chinese parsley, cilantro has flat, frilly leaves that resemble those of flat-leaf (Italian) parsley. Its flavor is pungent, slightly grassy, and a little astringent.

DILL

The sprightly taste of this feathery-leaved herb is lost when the leaves are dried or cooked, so buy the freshest dill you can find, with bright green leaves and stems, and add it to dishes just before serving.

MINT

This refreshingly sweet herb is a popular seasoning for lamb, poultry, vegetables, and fruit. Spearmint is the variety most commonly sold in food stores.

OREGANO

Also known as wild marjoram, this highly aromatic and spicy herb, a staple of Italian and Greek cooking, is used fresh or dried in all kinds of savory dishes and goes particularly well with tomatoes. Greek oregano is noteworthy for its pungent flavor.

PARSLEY

The flat-leaf, or Italian, variety of this widely popular fresh herb native to southern Europe is more pronounced in flavor than the common curly type, making it preferable as a seasoning.

ROSEMARY

Used either fresh or dried, this Mediterranean herb has an aromatic flavor well suited to meats, poultry, seafood, and vegetables. It is particularly popular as a seasoning for chicken or lamb.

SAGE

Soft, oval, gray-green sage leaves are pungent, sweet, and aromatic. Used both fresh and dried, they go especially well with poultry, vegetables, and pork.

THYME

One of the most important culinary herbs of Europe, thyme delivers a light fragrance and earthy, floral flavor to all types of food. Used both fresh and dried, it complements mild cheeses, vegetables, and meats.

NUTS

Nuts contribute their mellow taste and crunchy texture to both savory and sweet dishes. For the best selection, look in a specialty-food shop, health-food store, or the baking section of a food market. Some of the most popular options include **pine nuts,** the small, ivory-colored, resinous-tasting nuts extracted from the cones of a species of pine tree; and rich, crisp **walnuts,** of which the English variety is the most widely available.

OILS

Various good-quality oils are used in the Mediterranean kitchen. Nearly tasteless types such as **safflower oil, vegetable oil, corn oil,** or the somewhat richer **peanut oil** are excellent for all-purpose cooking. So, too, is **pure olive oil,** which has been blended and refined. **Extra-virgin olive oils,** by contrast, are generally fruity and full flavored, a reflection of the character of the olives from which they were pressed, and range in flavor from spicy and peppery to buttery and mellow. Use them for dressing salads or as a condiment. Buy **walnut** and **Asian sesame oils** in small quantities, as they tend to go rancid quickly.

OLIVES

Olives are cured in both their unripe green and ripened brownish to black forms, using various combinations of salt, seasonings, brines, vinegars, and oils. Good assortments of cured olives may be found in well-stocked food stores and delicatessens. Among those commonly available are Greek **Kalamata olives,** a pungent, brine-cured black variety packed in vinegar; and small, brownish black **Niçoise olives** from Provence. Crushed **pastes** of black olives, moistened with olive oil and sometimes seasoned with salt and herbs, are available sold in tubes and jars in many good delicatessens.

ONIONS

Onions of many kinds add pungency to the Mediterranean table. The varieties called for in this book include **green (spring) onions,** also known as scallions, which are long, slender white bulbs harvested immature, leaves and all; **red (Spanish) onions,** a mild, sweet variety with purplish red skin and red-tinged white flesh; and **yellow onions,** the most commonly available, distinguished by their dry, yellowish brown skins and strong-flavored white flesh.

PANCETTA

A specialty of the Emilia-Romagna region of northern Italy, this unsmoked bacon is cured with salt and pepper. It is sold either flat or rolled up into a cylinder, to be sliced and used to add a rich undertone of flavor to long-simmered dishes or stuffings. Look for pancetta in well-stocked food stores and Italian delicatessens.

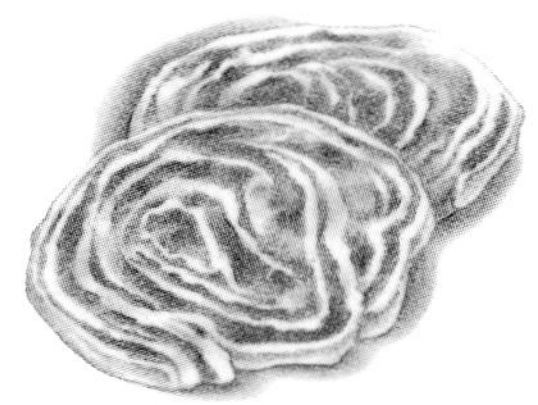

POLENTA

This term refers to both a specially ground Italian-style cornmeal and the mush that is cooked from it. Look in Italian delicatessens and well-stocked markets for regular Italian polenta, rather than the quick-cooking kind.

TAHINI

A specialty of the Middle East, this rich tan paste is ground from sesame seeds, to be used as an enrichment in both savory and sweet dishes. Tahini is commercially packaged in jars and cans and may be found in Middle Eastern markets and well-stocked food stores.

VINEGAR

The word *vinegar* literally means "sour wine," describing what results when certain strains of yeast cause wine or another flavorful liquid to ferment for a second time, turning it sharply acidic. The best-quality wine vinegars begin with good-quality wine. **Red wine vinegar,** like the wine from which it is made, has a more robust flavor than vinegar produced from white wine. **Sherry vinegar** is distinguished by the rich flavor and tawny color of the fortified, cask-aged wine from which it is made. Italian **balsamic vinegar,** a highly prized specialty of Modena and Reggio Emilia, starts with cooked and reduced grape juice, which is aged for many years in a progression of barrels made of different woods, to produce a vinegar of almost syruplike consistency, with a complex and intense flavor.

YOGURT, PLAIN

Noted for its mildly acidic flavor and custard-like texture, yogurt is made from lightly fermented milk. It adds mellow richness, body, and tang to a wide variety of both savory and sweet dishes.

SPICES

Derived from aromatic seeds, berries, buds, roots, or barks, a wide range of spices enlivens many Mediterranean foods.

ALLSPICE

This sweet Caribbean spice, sold ground or as whole dried berries, gets its name because its flavor resembles a blend of cinnamon, cloves, and nutmeg.

CAYENNE PEPPER

Finely ground from the dried cayenne chile, this orange-red powdered seasoning delivers a spicy-hot accent.

CINNAMON

One of the most popular sweet-hot spices, cinnamon is the aromatic bark of a type of evergreen tree, sold ground or in long, thin curls (cinnamon sticks).

CLOVES

Native to Southeast Asia, these dried flower buds of an evergreen tree have a highly aromatic flavor. They are used whole or ground in both sweet and savory recipes.

CORIANDER

The small, spicy-sweet seeds of the coriander plant, also the source of the herb known as fresh cilantro or Chinese parsley.

CUMIN

Sold either as whole seeds or ground into a pale brown powder, cumin is popular in Middle Eastern, Indian, and Mexican kitchens for its strong, dusky flavor and aroma.

NUTMEG

This popular baking spice is ground from the hard fruit pit of the nutmeg tree. For the best flavor, grate nutmeg as needed.

PAPRIKA

Made from the dried paprika pepper, this powdered spice is available in sweet, mild, and hot forms. Hungarian paprikas are generally considered to be the best quality.

RED PEPPER FLAKES

The coarsely crushed flesh and seeds of dried hot red chile, this seasoning adds a touch of fire to sauces and marinades.

SAFFRON THREADS

It takes the hairlike stigmas from many thousands of blossoms of a variety of crocus to yield 1 pound (500 g) of this golden, richly perfumed spice, one of the world's most expensive. Fortunately, just a pinch of saffron will impart a bright, sunny color and heady aroma to a dish. Look for saffron threads; saffron that has been ground loses its flavor more rapidly.

INDEX

ACKNOWLEDGMENTS

The publishers would like to thank the following people and associations for their generous support and assistance in producing this book: Linda Bouchard, Ken DellaPenta, Kathryn Meehan, Anna Preslar, Vivian Ross, and Hill Nutrition Associates.

The following kindly lent props for photography: Ma Maison, San Francisco, CA. The photographer would like to thank Tammy and Mark Becker for generously sharing their home for location photography. She would also like to thank ProCamera, San Francisco, CA; and FUJI film for their generous support of this project.